VOICES
in the
PINES

VOICES
in the
PINES

True Stories from the
New Jersey Pine Barrens

KAREN F. RILEY

Plexus Publishing, Inc.
Medford, New Jersey

Second Printing, July 2009

Voices in the Pines: True Stories from the New Jersey Pine Barrens

Copyright © 2009 by Karen F. Riley

Published by: Plexus Publishing, Inc.
                  143 Old Marlton Pike
                  Medford, NJ 08055

Library of Congress Cataloging-in-Publication Data

Riley, Karen F., 1962-
   Voices in the pines : true stories from the New Jersey Pine Barrens / Karen F. Riley.
       p. cm.
   Includes bibliographical references.
       ISBN: 978-0-937548-67-7
       1. Pine Barrens (N.J.)--History--Anecdotes. 2. Pine Barrens (N.J.)--Biography--Anecdotes. I. Title.
   F142.P5R55 2009
       974.9'61043—dc22

                                                                2009008819

Printed and bound in the United States of America.

President and CEO: Thomas H. Hogan, Sr.
Editor-in-Chief and Publisher: John B. Bryans
Managing Editor: Amy M. Reeve
VP Graphics and Production: M. Heide Dengler
Book Designer: Kara Mia Jalkowski
Cover Designer: Andrew Gioulis
Copyeditor: Bonnie Freeman
Proofreader: Barbara Brynko

Illustrations by Andrew Gioulis

www.plexuspublishing.com

To Bill, my soulmate and husband of 28 years.
Without you, this book would never have been written.
You are and always will be my inspiration for life.

CONTENTS

Acknowledgments

I have discovered that this is the hardest part of any book to write. There are so many great folks to thank, and I don't want to leave anyone out. Each and every individual I encountered in the process of researching and writing *Voices in the Pines* helped me to look at things in a new light.

If you are one of those who generously gave of your time to be interviewed but whose words do not appear in the book, please know that you had a real impact nonetheless. Your dedication, your beliefs, and your lifestyle helped to shape my view of the Pine Barrens and its respected denizens, the Pineys. Your words challenged me, caused me to move in new directions, and became a vital part of the book.

Certain individuals contributed in a large way to *Voices in the Pines,* and I am indebted to them for their efforts. First, there are three men who played vital roles in getting the book into your hands.

It all starts with a dream, and that dream was hatched in the back of the room at the initial signing and talk for my first book, *Whispers in the Pines: The Secrets of Colliers Mills.* My husband, Bill Riley, along for moral support, soaked in the questions and comments of the people who had gathered there. Bill is adept at "reading between the lines," and the recurring theme he picked up on was: What about the people behind that history?

Bill was right, and at almost every book signing since, at least one person has asked me about the people of the Pine Barrens. Let's face it: Some of us like history more than others, but we all enjoy stories about real people. We're social beings at our very core. And so the idea for this book was born: to bring Pinelands history alive through the eyes of the people who live it every day.

Bill sat through many lonely weekends as I traversed the region, meeting and talking with the people and, in some cases, accompanying them on their daily routines. He suffered through missed (and cold) meals, my writing late into the night, and having to be "very quiet" while I worked. He did it all without complaint—honestly. I know how truly blessed I am to have such a man by my side. Thank you, Bill, for your love and unconditional support.

Next, thanks go to my editor, John B. Bryans of Plexus Publishing, Inc. I first met John at a book signing in Whitesbog Village, sponsored by the Pinelands Preservation Alliance. We talked about my idea for a second book, and he was extremely encouraging. I urge all writers to look for a publisher who understands and supports their dream—that's the best chance for it to be effectively brought to print.

With the explosion in self-publishing options, just about anyone who ever got an A on a third-grade composition seems to fancy himself or herself a writer these days, but the reality is that writing a book is only one part of the equation. It takes an understanding of marketing, distribution, production, and many other facets of the publishing process to get a book into the hands of those readers who may have a sincere interest in it. Thank you, John, for believing in me and in my dream.

The third member of this trio is Andrew Gioulis. Andrew is my business partner in my 9-to-5 world, but he was also my partner in making this book come alive. Some authors and publishers merely hire a fine illustrator; I was blessed to have one who worked with this dream from its inception. Just as Bill kept the home fires burning (and the floors washed and the dishes done), Andrew kept the business going while the book pulled me in other directions. Always curious, his ears perked up the first time I used the word *Piney*. He wanted to learn about these folks and their lifestyles, and thus, he accompanied me to many of the interviews and heard the stories firsthand. His illustrations at the beginning of each chapter help bring the narrative to life.

I am reminded of my interview with Niki Giberson and how her husband, Gary, never let her settle for anything less than her very best in her work. Andrew has always done the same for me in our business and now in this book, and I am the better for it. Thank you, Andrew, for your honesty, your commitment, and your talent.

There are so many other tremendous people out there I want to thank: managing editor, Amy Reeve, who was always there with her upbeat personality and helpful suggestions; my best friend, Maryann Kley, whose unlimited patience with me has endured the tests of time and distance; the gang at the Jackson Writers Group, who encouraged and guided me; the folks who prayed for me; and the unsung heroes who work in New Jersey's historical societies, libraries, nonprofits, and many other types of groups and organizations. Each of you has been woven somewhere into the fabric of this book. May you continue to brightly color the world of those around you.

Last, but certainly not least, I want to thank the great men and women of the Pines—many of whom are no longer with us. You believed in the dream and kept it alive, and I am honored to call you Pineys. May your spirit continue to be renewed in the ever-changing seasons of the Pines.

Foreword

The New Jersey Pinelands, with the Pine Barrens as its core, is one of the most fascinating places on the eastern seaboard of the United States. It doesn't have gorgeous mountain vistas or expanses of ocean stretching out to the sunrise, but it is enchanting nevertheless.

Deep within the Pine Barrens are dark swamps, sand roads that have been traversed since the early days of settlement and some even before that, little rivers—that would be called creeks anywhere else—that flow with the dark and silky tannin-stained waters of the lowland swamps. In night's obscurity, the camper and hiker finds a taste of the fear with which early Europeans faced the endless forests of this new world. Coyotes and black bears roam the woods, though, thankfully, the cougar has not been reintroduced.

Long-abandoned village sites are found throughout the pines, and cellar holes of homes that no longer ring with the laughter of children are the only remains of the vibrant human life that once called the Pine Barrens home. Women took care of their homes and toiled in gardens that have returned to forest. Sand roads are prolific, but many don't go anywhere anymore. Their destinations are only clearings now. Once there were grist mills and lumber mills, furnaces, forges, and paper mills. Men worked in cedar mining, charcoal making, ship-building, glass making, and other local industries that made the land throb with life. Today, there is silence.

During the eighteenth and nineteenth centuries, sailing ships carried the products of the pines down rivers to the sea, and the industries that made those products stripped the land of its forests and drained its swamps. Yes, by today's standards, the settlers exploited the land; they did so to feed their children, but they also loved that land and called it their own for generations.

There were poor people left out in the woods after the industries in which they worked died. There were college-educated people who still chose to return to the land of their birth. There were sailors and sea captains who farmed when they weren't out sailing.

Even today, the residents of the Pine Barrens love their land with its solitude and peace. The land itself still produces. The cranberry and blueberry farmers are stewards of their realm and know how precious the water is to those who live in the area. Other area denizens may work outside the area but still return to the towns that nourished their ancestors.

Colorful people and wonderful stories yet thrive in this area that is so very different from the surrounding megalopolis. Historians and writers like Arthur Pierce, Henry Charlton Beck, John McPhee, and I spent many years collecting the stories of present and past that the essence of this special world might be preserved for the future. The dedication of my book was sincerely made to all those people of the pines who were truly the "heart of the pines."

Once again, another writer has been seduced by the enticing pinelands. Karen Riley took pen to paper that she might ramble through that "heart" yet again with those who continue to love and labor in the pines in this 21st century. Their stories are fascinating, just as the stories told by those who came before them.

Many of those whom she interviewed are familiar to me. Others are not. Yet every story is special. Even though I no longer live in New Jersey, Ms. Riley took me back to a place and a people that I still love very much. She has found what I found before her: Once you meet the people and walk the walk of the Pines, you just get drawn in to a love of the place. The spirit envelops you, and you are home as you never expected to be.

So sit back and meet the people of the Pines today, varied and interesting as they have always been, but be careful. You, too, may be hooked on the Pines.

—John Pearce
Heart of the Pines:
Ghostly Voices of the Pine Barrens

Introduction

It was a clear, cloudless July day. The year was 2001. I leaned over the rail and watched the Atlantic Ocean churn in the wake of the ferry. I looked back at the six girls charged to my care that day, ranging in age from 15 to 17. They were from Florida, Maine, Iowa, and California. One was polite, another shy; another looked as if she could be trouble. The thing they shared was that this was their first time in New Jersey and New York.

Our New Jersey Girl Scout Council sponsored its first Wider Opportunity that year, carefully selecting 80 girls from around the world who wanted to experience firsthand what this part of the country had to offer. Volunteers all took a turn at chaperoning on different days, and I was excited to be accompanying them on their trip to New York.

We were headed for the Statue of Liberty, and I pointed out the familiar silhouettes across New York Harbor to the girls, who jockeyed back and forth among the crowd for the best position to get photographs. "That's the Empire State Building, there's the Chrysler Building, and those are the Twin Towers."

I sighed as I looked at those familiar steel spires and remembered my days working in the Grand Concourse. When I lived in the city, I made many trips to the observation deck and the roof three floors higher.

I recalled the afternoon I spent studying the map outlines on the glass windows of the observation deck, learning the names of unfamiliar buildings that played a role in the city's history. That day I stayed until closing, watching the sun set as it cast long orange streaks across the slanted steel roofs. Then, little by little, the lights came on in the tiny office windows across the city. I thought about one of New York's nicknames—the city that never sleeps—and how appropriate it was. As New Yorkers scurried home to have dinner with their families, the second shift was just starting its workday.

It had been several years since I had been to the Twin Towers, now that we were living in New Jersey. I made a promise to take my kids there in late September, after they were back in school and the tourists had left. It was a promise I was unable to keep.

***

In his book *The Pine Barrens*, John McPhee wrote, "It would appear that the Pine Barrens are not very likely to be the subject of dramatic decrees or acts of legislation. They seem to be headed slowly towards extinction."[1] These words tore at the heart of Governor Brendan Byrne, who set out to find a way to prevent the extinction. Thus, the New Jersey Pinelands Commission was born.

We all take things for granted in our lives and just assume they will always be there. Sometimes we don't even take the time to explore what's beyond our own backyards.

***

I was sitting in Lucille's Country Cooking diner in Warren Grove, chatting with the owner, Lucille Bates-Wickward. She told me how she learned something new every day from her customers. In this way, she was able to travel around the world without ever leaving her diner.

She asked me where I grew up, and I told her about playing in the concrete backyards and alleyways of Brooklyn, New York. How those alleyways, surrounded by apartment buildings, meant I always had a hundred pairs of eyes watching my every step—dozens of "mothers" to make sure I stayed out of trouble. How we played skully on the sidewalks, delineating boxes with colored chalk at which to aim our bottlecaps. In the summer, I would stay out until it got dark, then come home dirty and tired but happy.

Lucille and I talked for hours, and I got to know about her life and her diner. As I was leaving, she reminded me, "See, I learn something new every day from my customers." With a smile, she continued, "And today I traveled to Brooklyn and saw alleyways where kids played tag and hide-and-seek. I got to see Brooklyn today, through your eyes."

***

My dad made a point of taking me all over the city. He told me that it was important to know about the place in which you lived. When you traveled outside the area, you should be able to tell people what it was like back home. I didn't know it then, but he was instilling in me pride for my roots.

We traveled to Manhattan by subway, and I learned that avenues run north and south, streets east and west. If you are walking on an avenue and the street numbers increase, you are headed north.

He took me to Queens, where he was born and raised. We went to Staten Island and acted as if Clove Lakes Park was the country. For a city kid, it *was* the country. There wasn't a lot of green acreage where I grew up. I came home exhausted from climbing the hilly terrain the day we went to the Bronx Zoo.

By the time I reached high school, I had a plan. I hung a subway map up in my room and marked off the routes I had traveled. By graduation, I planned to ride every train line in the New York City subway system, all 660 miles. I didn't quite make it, but I came close.

When my husband, our three kids, and I moved to New Egypt, New Jersey, we made a plan to get to know our new home the way we knew our old one. On the weekends, we would take different routes and explore the surrounding towns.

Later on, I would take my car down sugar sand roads and check out the Pine Barrens. There was something about the fresh, clean air, the scraggly pitch pines, and the unexpected creeks around the bend in the road that called my name. This was a rich treasure, and I wanted to learn everything there was to know about it.

***

I have had the privilege of meeting many people who make their living and their homes in the Pine Barrens. Some have been here for generations; others are "transplants" who have come to love this area as much as I have.

Our roots will always be the places closest to our hearts; they are what has colored our vision and influenced our ideas as we grew up. It's the reason we all laugh at forwarded emails that begin, "You know you are from New Jersey [or wherever] when …"—we know our past has shaped who we have become.

Take us out of our element and we can adapt, but we will never know our new home the way we did our old. If we are lucky, we can work at letting it grow in our hearts alongside the old memories.

We recognize that others appear different to us—their accents, their mannerisms, sometimes how they walk or do things. We often forget that we are just as different to them—and we are now the visitors to their home.

Sometimes it's hard to imagine how others feel when they are on our home turf. I spent a wonderful morning with Newt Sterling of

Port Republic. Newt is a Piney—an individual who makes a living off the land in the Pine Barrens. He is considered by many to be one of the best snaremen, or trappers, in the world. He traps year-round, in swamps and in snow, in the thick of woods and in open fields. He walks among coyotes and black bear and trudges through creeks and streams with muskrat and snapping turtles. None of this fazes him. But Newt had the opportunity to travel to New York City several years ago—and he told me you couldn't pay him enough to go back to the concrete jungle.

If we are open-minded, we can learn from our differences and discover what we have in common. We can laugh good-naturedly at what sets us apart rather than deride those whose backgrounds are different from ours. We can come to recognize humanity as a majestic tapestry woven from diverse experiences and cultures.

***

In the western part of the Pine Barrens sits a tiny little town nestled among the pines. Settlers came to this area in 1778 and built a log cabin church. Under the guidance of Presbyterian minister John Brainerd, the church became known as the Tabernacle in the Wilderness. Back then, church was often the center of community life, and the town became known as Tabernacle.

Lifetime resident Frank Ingram wrote a great poem to commemorate Tabernacle's Centennial Celebration. He was gracious enough to allow me to share his words here:

> You're from where? said he with a mystified look and a
> questioning eye
> Tabernacle, said I, where the air is still and the earth
> meets the sky
> Isn't that "out in the sticks" he said?

If by "out in the sticks" you mean far removed from the
   madness of city living, I say yes
Do you know what it means to live "out in the sticks"?
Away from the jumble of concrete and bricks
To wake up in the morning to the sounds of birds
And the deer running by in miniature herds.
To live in a town where your neighbor's your friend
And the peace and the quiet go on without end
Do you know how it feels to sit back in your chair
And fill your nostrils with clean country air?
Watch a butterfly's flight or a bird on the wing
A town founded by faith in the Lord and the land
From the Tabernacle in the Wilderness near where we
   now stand
The church may be gone but the faith still remains
Tabernacle today is still much the same
We're still a small town as most towns go
And our children still frolic midst the pines in the snow
Imagine counting the stars at night
Do you know how it feels to enjoy such a sight?
From Emilio Carranza to Indian Ann
We're proud of our soil on which we stand
We're one hundred years young and we've seen the best
   and worst of times
We'll be here for the next hundred years in our Gateway
   to the Pines.[2]

***

Children tend to transplant more easily than adults do. After we
had been down here a year, I took one of my daughters with me to
visit Brooklyn. She was 9 at the time. We found her best friend from

childhood, the one she spent every summer day with. There was never any level of discomfort between them. But now, with a year and 50 miles separating them, the silence was awkward. They struggled to bridge the gap of time and distance. After what seemed like an agonizing few minutes, my daughter decided to break the ice. "Seen any deer lately?" she asked innocently. I knew she had adjusted, perhaps too well.

***

Coming from my Brooklyn roots to the wilds of Toms River, I can understand how it must have felt for Cowboy Joe. He worked as a DJ for radio station WOBM, broadcasting out of Berkeley Township.

One winter night in 1968, two young police officers, Bill Sneddon and Bob Kruysman, stopped by. Back then, there really weren't any places open late at night, and WOBM always kept a pot of hot coffee going in the lobby.

Bill isn't sure if it was the late hour or the coffee, but when Cowboy Joe asked, "So what do you boys do for fun around here?" he replied, without missing a beat, "Well, there's the Wells Mills Frog Farm."

"What's that?" Cowboy asked, his curiosity piqued.

"Well, we go out on the lake and dredge for frogs."

"How many do you catch?"

"Too many."

"How big are they?"

"Oh, about 10 to 20 pounds. They live off those big Jersey mosquitoes, you know."

I could just picture Cowboy's face. After all, New Yorkers refer to mosquitoes as New Jersey's state bird.

Bill and Bob had just been passing the time. They didn't really give the Wells Mills Frog Farm much of a second thought, but they mentioned the visit later to their friends Cliff Oakley and Toby Spratt. Cliff thought the story was too good to get away.

So Cliff went to Clayton's Restaurant in Barnegat, near the corner of Route 72, and ordered gourmet frog legs. He wrapped them in tin foil and delivered them to Cowboy Joe, along with a bottle of French wine. (He did not know at the time that Cowboy had a problem with alcohol.)

Cowboy Joe was loaded with questions now. Cliff asked if Cowboy would play some Eddie Arnold songs in return for Cliff's answering the questions. Cowboy agreed.

He told Cowboy how they packed the frogs, six to a box, and shipped them to the Fulton Fish Market in New York City, knowing that Cowboy would be familiar with the famous city market.

"We're religious people," Cliff warned him. "Never fish on a Sunday, never frog on a Sunday." Then he told Cowboy about Toby.

"One day, we were frogging, and we caught this extra-large frog, and we weighed him, and he was 27 pounds, which was extra large for New Jersey. Very nice frog, very well-behaved frog, well-groomed, took care of himself. … We named him Toby.

"We put him on a chain, put a collar on, gave him a little water, caught some mosquitoes for him, put them in a pan, and all went to bed. When we got up the next morning, the chain was broke and Toby was gone. Well, it wasn't too much later and I got a call from Mrs. Justy in Brookville, and she had just seen Toby go over her clothesline."

Bill Sneddon eventually became chief of police. He retired in 1999 and lives in Waretown. Bob Kruysman has retired to Florida. Cliff Oakley has life rights to the Wells Mills cabin, where he has lived since he was 18. The land was purchased in 1936 and is now part of the Ocean County Parks Department. Cliff works part-time as a park ranger at the Wells Mills County Park. His cabin sits alongside the lake in which the four men had gone frogging many years ago.

Even though Cowboy Joe no longer works for WOBM and the story has been forgotten by some, there are others who still remember Toby. Cliff told me, "We had some Boy Scouts up this summer, and they said they saw Toby up by the lake. I went up to look for him, but I couldn't find him."

Cliff still keeps Toby's broken chain in his cabin as a memory. "I never saw Toby again. Apparently, he is still alive, but we don't know for sure."

Endnotes

1. John McPhee, *The Pine Barrens* (New York: Farrar, Strauss and Giroux, 1967), 156.
2. Frank Ingram, "Untitled Poem," in *Tabernacle Township Centennial Celebration* (Tabernacle, NJ: Tabernacle Township, 2001).

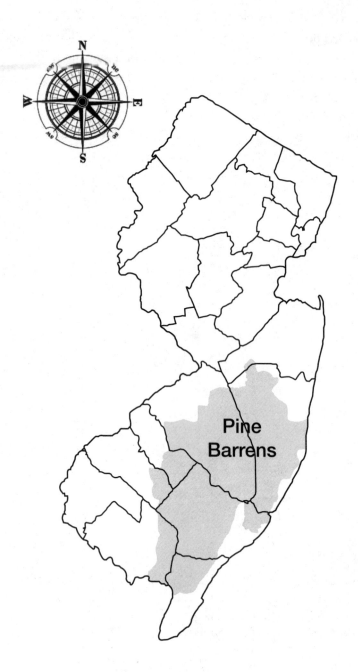

Pine
Barrens

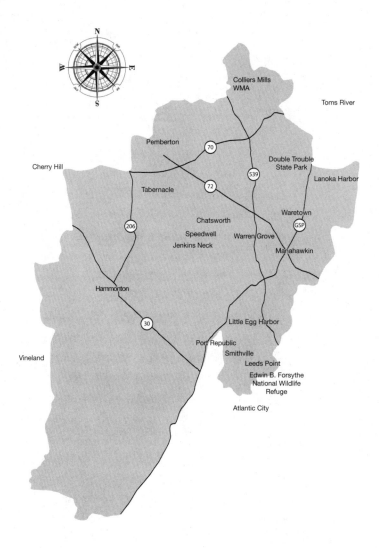

Colliers Mills
WMA

Toms River

Pemberton

70

Double Trouble
State Park

Cherry Hill

539

Lanoka Harbor

Tabernacle

72

Chatsworth

Waretown

206

Speedwell

Warren Grove

GSP

Jenkins Neck

Manahawkin

Hammonton

30

Little Egg Harbor

Port Republic

Vineland

Smithville

Leeds Point

Edwin B. Forsythe
National Wildlife
Refuge

Atlantic City

Cape May

Murder in the Pines

The scene replayed itself almost every night. As soon as Barry climbed the stairs to his room on the second floor of the old farmhouse, he felt the eerie presence. He would slide under the covers and hug Donny, his black Labrador-cocker spaniel mix, tight. He listened to the birds call outside his window, their claws clattering against the gutter as they landed on the roof. He was used to these sounds at night. But there was something else, something heavy that hung in the silence within his room.

And then it would come. Barry would squeeze his eyes shut. After a few moments, his 6-year-old mind filled with curiosity, and he would cautiously raise his eyelids a crack. In the beams of moonlight that streamed through his window, he could make out a shadow approaching. His eyes opened with fright as the shadow's presence seemed to fill the room.

The dark shadow hovered over him. It was too much for young Barry. "Daddy! Daddy! Help me, it's going to get me!" Barry screamed out in terror. He could scarcely catch his breath.

His father came into the bedroom, turned on the light, and reassured Barry. "It's OK, you're just having a nightmare again, Barry. See, there's nothing here." Barry tried to let his father's words calm him. After all, his father was big and strong and surely able to handle anything that threatened to hurt him.

Barry's parents had purchased the farm a few years before he was born. His dad, Howard Steinmetz, was a World War II vet. He had been intrigued by the stories of the soldiers he bunked beside in boot camp. One was a dairy farmer with seven cows; another was a poultry farmer who owned a thousand chickens. Howard vowed that he would become a farmer after he got home from the service.

Although the nation was prospering after World War II, jobs were still hard to come by for a young veteran in Kingston, New York. Howard accepted work in a slaughterhouse, then a trucking firm, and finally alongside his father, Benjamin Steinmetz, building houses by hand and selling them for a profit.

In his declining years, Benjamin traded a house and some property in Kingston for 500 acres of farmland in Warren Grove, New Jersey, sight unseen. Father and son traveled down to Warren Grove in 1955; Howard hoped to start a farm for himself and his young bride, Agnes. The two farms he had looked at in Kingston were out of his price range.

They arrived at the property alongside Simm Place Road and were taken with its beauty. A picturesque lake stretched out before them. Birch and other pioneer trees lined its edges, a sign of nature's progress in reclaiming former cranberry bogs. As the men located the rock that marked the property's corner boundary, they felt Benjamin had made a good trade. The father and son headed into Mt. Holly to record the deed since Warren Grove was part of Burlington County at the time.

When they got there, they were told the deed was bogus; the owner had been duplicating and "selling" it over and over again. For years, they tried every avenue to claim the land, to no avail. In the meantime, Howard was growing restless. During one of their stays, he discovered Tuckerton to the south—a very small town at the time. He became enchanted with the bay; it reminded him of the water near Throgs Neck, where he grew up. "My dad and I love sailing," Barry told me. "Once it gets in your blood, you just can't give it up."

Howard talked to area real estate agents, and Granville Price in Tuckerton told him about the Sands property. It was an abandoned 10-acre poultry farm just off Mathistown Road in Little Egg Harbor. What attracted Howard to the farm—apart from the price—was the coop capacity. Heavily encumbered, the property was put on the block and sold at a sheriff's sale in Toms River around 1956. Howard offered more than the other bidder—$6,000—and this covered the tax lien and all the debt.

When Howard and Agnes arrived on the Sands property with the moving van, the horse and cow that had been left there were gone; someone had stolen them. Weeds were waist high in the fields, and the farm was overrun with insects, bats, rats, and mice. The farmhouse had been vandalized, and there were dried bloodstains on the kitchen floor. Barry remembered that his mother was so upset by the condition of the property and the house that she talked his father into putting a For Sale sign on the property. His father did—but for a very high speculator's price—as he had every intention of turning someone else's nightmare into his dream farm.

Howard got busy repairing the damage to the house as Agnes scrubbed the floors and made it livable again. He took down the windmill that stood alongside the house, deeming it a magnet for lightning. He bought an old tractor and poured oil and coolant into it each day to replace what had leaked out. He purchased a 7-foot mower that had been used to trim the edges alongside the Garden State Parkway. He hitched it behind the tractor to plow the fields and cut down the weeds.

The pride of the farm was a 200-foot coop, in which Howard installed an automatic feeder and waterer that Barry said was revolutionary for a poultry farm in the mid-1950s. "The feed company would bring a big Mack truck," Barry recalled. "They would dump off these big sacks of cracked corn and feed, and my dad would dump them into the hopper, and it would distribute it out 200 feet." Behind this main coop were two smaller, 100-foot coops.

The walls of the coops were framed out with wood standing four feet high, and the floors were simple cement slabs. At the front was a wide screen for ventilation. The windows—actually just open space between the walls and roof—were covered with quarter-inch chicken wire mesh and barbed wire to discourage varmints, as the Steinmetz family called them. The windows were kept open year-round because, as Howard told me, "If you try to keep chickens warm, they get sick and die. They are OK with drafts; chicken feathers are some of the warmest material around. That's why they use it for coats and blankets."

The Steinmetzes were able to put about 250 chickens in each pen, allowing each chicken four square feet of living space, which was necessary to prevent fighting among the chickens. Howard told me that chickens will fight and peck each other to death—which is where the term *pecking order* originated. "It is very noisy in the coop; chickens do a lot of talking. But as soon as it gets dark, they go up on their roosts and sleep."

Howard would buy baby chicks and raise them with brooder stoves, which simulated the warmth of the hen's feathers and would keep the chicks warm. Each stove could handle about 500 chicks, and the number of stoves you owned determined how many chicks you could raise.

After about 17 weeks, the chicks would start laying eggs, and they would produce an average of one egg per day for months until they went into molt and stopped laying. "Molt is when the primary feather falls out," Barry explained.

"You had the expense of feeding them through the molt, when they weren't producing, into the next laying season, or you could call the butcher to come pick up the thousands of chicks you had in molt so you didn't have to keep feeding them," Howard told me. "I did it both ways—it was just as good to feed them through the molt as to sell them and start off with new baby chicks. Either way, we constantly had eggs."

Howard explained that when you keep only hens that are producing, it is known as having an all-pullet farm, *pullet* referring to a young, laying chicken. They kept only hens on the farm—no roosters—so they never had to worry about fertilized eggs. Once eggs are fertilized, you cannot sell them for food, only as future chickens.

Every morning, Howard and Agnes would start their routine by feeding the chickens, washing out the fountains, and making sure that all the chickens had fresh water. Then they would collect the eggs and change the litter. On Monday mornings, they would deliver the eggs along their route. The rest of the week, they stayed on the farm and took care of business, including the customers who stopped by to purchase eggs.

When Barry got older, he assisted his parents with the farm chores. "I remember putting my hand under the chicken and pulling the egg out. They would peck at me; they didn't like me touching their eggs. Then you had to carry them in a basket into the house. It was a lot of work, and there was a lot of walking involved. My dad had to wear boots because of all the manure.

"We would collect eggs in a wire basket and bring them into the basement, where they were immersed in a washing machine. The machine used a special soap to clean the feces and dirt off the egg," Barry remembered. "The basement had 2-by-12 beams, and my dad drove nails into them and hung the baskets of washed eggs up to dry."

The eggs were then candled and put in an egg-grading unit. "It would weigh the eggs and put them down different slots for different sizes," Howard explained. "The weight of the egg determines if it is large, medium, or small. Believe it or not, eggs are sold by weight, not size. But of course, a large egg not only weighs more but is larger than a medium egg, and so on. Government regulations specify that eggs have to be weighed on a scale and graded."

Barry explained candling to me: "In the old days, they used a candle, but we had a light bulb that came with the egg-grading unit. You would hold the egg up against a light bulb, and it would show you exactly what's inside the egg. You can do this with any egg today by holding it up to the light. If there's any blood or any cracks, you put the egg off to the side. One of my joys was that at the end of the night, I got to throw those eggs that were put on the side. I was the king of egg chucking. I would throw them out the back cellar and let them fly like hand grenades."

Another word in the poultry farming vernacular is *culling*, as in separating out the less appropriate chickens. Certain chickens were deemed *culls* by their coop mates. "That would be the chicken that is deprived of food and water; that would be the one my dad would have to throw out," Barry said. "I don't know why they would pick on this one chicken, and you couldn't do anything about it—it would just happen. My dad would try to move that chicken to another area, but it would happen again. The chickens seem to know when there is a weakling amongst them. They are just very cruel in that respect; they would just deprive that chicken of a chance to get water and food. It's sad."

Barry's father would then remove the chicken from the coop and leave it out on its own, where it would soon be taken by another animal for food. "There was always death; farms are all about death," Barry said, adding that "everything was a cycle, and nothing ever went to waste." However, sometimes the cycle got interrupted. "Donny would often find the rejected chicken, and he would very carefully pick it up in his mouth—he would never hurt it—and bring it back to the coop because he knew it didn't belong out. My dad would wave at him and say, 'No, no, Donny, that one has to stay out.'"

Donny was Barry's constant companion. The two would go into the woods behind the house and hunt for discarded bottles among the piles of leaves. Barry unearthed an impressive collection of Coke bottles, medicine bottles, and perfume bottles near foundations where houses once stood. The Coke bottles had thick bottoms with dates on them and corks instead of screw caps.

Donny shared his living quarters with the family's 32 cats and considered himself one of them. He would lie on the floor at Agnes's feet as the cats would climb on him and slide down his shiny fur. Agnes gave him the name *Donny* because she said his suave nature made her think of Don Juan.

Every day, Donny would wander over to the neighbor's house and wait on the porch as the woman put a bowl of milk down for her cats. When the last one had finished drinking, Donny would go over and lap up the rest. The neighbor said he was the most polite dog she had ever seen.

But when a woodchuck or stray dog would wander onto the Steinmetz's farm, Donny sprang into action. The veterinarian had to double-muzzle him each time he patched Donny up from his latest skirmish. Howard had trained Donny to keep animals away from his chicken coops, and Donny would, regardless of the size of the invader. All manner and type of animal wandered onto the property, from snakes slithering through the weeds to deer cutting through on their way to the swamp. Donny would take them all on. "The windows were all scratched up from Donny's nails when he was inside and heard something approaching," Barry said.

"When the deer hunters would come on our property, Donny would bark, and my dad would have to go out there with his gun and confront them. There was a lot of poaching. My dad would tell the authorities, but they would tell him that he wasn't going to be able to stop the people from hunting there as they have done it for years and years. They said they would talk to the hunters about staying away from the coops as it frightened the chickens and affected their laying.

"I almost got shot on that farm," Barry told me somberly. "Our next-door neighbors did not like my dad because he was an outsider, and our customers would drive past these neighbors' house on the way to ours because it had road frontage and we didn't. When the neighbors put their house up for sale, they refused to sell it to my dad and sold it to someone else, who made our lives even more miserable.

"There were two roads to get back to our property, and the new neighbor wanted to close one of the roads, but my dad refused. He wanted to keep both of them open for customers and in case of fire. The neighbor put a huge pile of dirt toward the back of the property [to block the road nearest to his house]. One day, one of his men took a .22-caliber rifle and was shooting into the dirt, toward our farm.

"I was playing outside by one of the coops, and I heard the bullet whiz by and explode the wood of the coop near me," Barry recalls. "I went running inside and told my dad. He called the cops, but the neighbor said it had only been an accident."

Many customers would stop by the farm. "When the people came in from the city, you would see the car doors open, and the kids would be running all over the place to see the chickens and the livestock and everything," Barry said. "People were enjoying the atmosphere as well as buying a good, fresh farm egg."

Besides selling eggs and poultry, the Steinmetz family also raised crops. "My dad grew what I thought was an amazing thing—a grape arbor that you could actually walk in. He made it like a square box. Concord grapes grew on the vines, and he would attach them to old cedar trees that he posthole-dug into the ground. There were four posts, a back, and sides. You would walk into it and eat grapes—the fattest, juiciest grapes I ever tasted in my whole life. He sent away for the Concord grape root through the mail. The customers would love it—we had one customer who came from Persia; he wanted the leaves to use in his cooking.

"My dad would also sell peach trees. He would go down to the farm markets and buy a nice, good, delicious peach. We'd eat the peach, but we would save the pits and put them along the foundation of the house. The pits would automatically go down into the ground after a time and start making little peach trees. My dad would take these little peach trees and set them out in a line and then sell them for $2 apiece. The people would rave about the peach trees. They would grow and have such delicious-tasting peaches because back then—in the 1960s—they weren't doing cross-breeding, and you would get a pure peach. Nowadays it would be very hard to take a peach pit because of its being altered. Once you start altering it, it doesn't grow correctly."

Howard bought White Leghorn chickens for laying and Rhode Island Reds, Barred Rocks, and Plymouth Rocks both for laying and as broilers. The dark hens laid a beautiful, brown, very large egg, according to Howard, and they yielded tender meat when their laying days were over.

He put signs out on Mathistown Road and Route 9 that read "Farm-Fresh Eggs for Sale and Poultry." Every Monday morning, he and Agnes would set out in their station wagon, bound for New Gretna, Mystic Island, and Tuckerton Beach to deliver farm-fresh eggs to the residents.

With every sale, Howard would say to his customers, "I would appreciate it if you would tell your friends and neighbors about the farm-fresh eggs and chicken," and they did. The passage of 50 years had not seemed to dampen his enthusiasm as he recited his sales pitch to me.

"You gotta understand, back in those days everybody knew each other, and word of mouth was one of the biggest ways of doing business," Howard explained. "If they said there was a cracked egg, I would give them two eggs extra. In those days, people were very honest, and when they told me something like that, I knew they weren't making it up."

After Barry was born, Howard and Agnes would take him along on their runs. Barry shared some of those memories with me. "The customers looked forward to seeing my dad; in fact, we had this one customer—she was so funny. Back then, a dozen eggs was under a dollar, but if my dad had to raise the price a few cents because the cost of buying the food for the chickens or the cost of the egg box went up, this lady—her name was Mitzy—would call out, 'Howard, where is your mask and gun?' And we always knew it was Mitzy, 'giving it' to Dad.

"Captain Mathis was a retired ship captain in Tuckerton. I remember he had a long driveway that went behind the house, and they had this little Scottie dog. The dog would never relent, my dad was always the burglar to him, and they always knew Howard was here. My dad would yell out, 'Egg man!' but the little dog would never give him a break; for years, he was always the bandit."

Howard's dad had taken correspondence courses and earned an engineering degree. He passed this knowledge and these skills on to his son. Barry said, "I think he taught my dad a lot about how to modernize and how to make do with what you had, because if my dad would have hired help like the other farmers did in the area, he would not have been able to make a profit on his egg business. My dad always told me that the profit on a dozen eggs was in the cents. It blew my mind that you could make a living with just making a few cents on a dozen eggs, but when you get done figuring out the cost of feed and the cost of electricity, because this thing was all electrified, it added up." The Steinmetzes never hired any help; they did all the work themselves and paid for everything in cash.

***

Every Friday, Barry's parents went shopping, and he would be alone from the time he got home from Little Egg Harbor Elementary School until late in the evening. "The kids in school would tell me that someone had been killed in my house before we moved there and would ask me if I was afraid. I would tell them that I felt that there was an evil presence in the house. I was always deathly afraid to be in that house by myself."

Barry asked his father on a few occasions about the stories the other kids would tell him about the house. His dad would tell him not to pay any attention to the stories and just ignore them. Barry tried to put the darkness out of his mind. As long as Donny was by his side, Barry was not as afraid.

Barry was only 9 years old when Donny died from heartworm. Barry recalled, "If you gave him a clean thing of water to drink out of, he wouldn't touch it; he preferred to drink out of a mud puddle, and of course in the mud were all the larvae." The veterinarian told Barry's father that he couldn't do anything for Donny and wanted to put him to sleep. "I remember my dad saying, 'Donny is like my son, and I will not put him to sleep. He will die a natural death.'" So Donny came home and died "a horrible death," according to Barry. His father buried Donny on the farm, alongside the cats that had died.

"The chickens would attract mice and rats with their feed like it was nobody's business," Barry said. "Even the 32 cats we had couldn't handle all that; it was overwhelming. My mother said she wore out can openers trying to feed all the cats. So my dad had to use a lot of traps. You couldn't use poison because if you used poison—which he tried at one point—it could get into the cats. He lost a lot of cats that ate mice that had already been poisoned."

After Donny's death, Barry would wander through the cold, empty house alone on Friday nights while his parents shopped. Howard kept a 12-gauge shotgun and a .22-caliber Marlin small-bore action rifle in the gun rack. "My dad always warned me, 'Do not touch the guns; they are deadly,' and he stored the ammunition away near the attic, where I couldn't reach it." But Barry would stretch out his hand and stroke the guns' smooth exteriors, it made him feel better to know they were there even though he knew they weren't loaded. "You got your guns through Sears Roebuck—through the catalog—they'd come through the mail," Barry explained. "It was disarmed; it couldn't fire until you put it all together. They sent it to you in pieces.

"We dealt with a lot of varmints on the farm," Barry recalled. "Mostly the weasels—extremely tough little animals. They would come up on the screening to kill the chicken and eat it and wouldn't leave until my dad came up behind them and clubbed them. We had tons of snakes on the farm; my dad had to shoot the snakes. I don't think my dad knew if they were poisonous or not. My dad wasn't taking any chances; he tried to move them, he tried to get them to leave, but they just wouldn't go. The farm had been abandoned for so long, they thought it was their home, and they were not going to move. Somebody had to give—my dad had the shotgun, and they gave. Unfortunately, on a farm, a shotgun and a .22 are your biggest tools against the varmints."

Howard cited two other varmints that Barry hadn't mentioned. "Raccoons are a big threat. And ferrets are a very dangerous animal to have on the farm—they're lethal killing machines. They'll kill chickens like crazy if they get in your coop. One time I lost 13 hens in one night, all because there was a hole in the bottom of the coop. I think the ferret made the hole to get to the birds. It wouldn't have been bad if he'd just killed one chicken and ate it, but he killed 13 hens and didn't eat nothin' to talk about other than their crop. A 12-gauge is a good friend of the farmer."

Howard and Barry also recalled the bugs they had on the farm. "You had to dress like it was wintertime—night and day, there were bugs," Howard said. "I counted 27 different biting insects one time."

"Anybody who tells me today that it's buggy out in the woods or the country has never grown up near Mystic Island," Barry told me. "Sandy Miller—who developed Mystic Island and Mystic Shores—drained the old oak swamp and got rid of all that stagnant water. We had so many bugs, mosquitoes, and gnats—it was just horrible. It would be like a black cloud.

"You actually had to run and go into the house through the basement because when you were in the dark, they couldn't find you to get in the house. The township had an old Willys jeep pickup with an amber light—the dome on the top—that would twirl around. It had a box on the back of the pickup truck that blew out blue smoke—kerosene and an insecticide, probably DDT or something very toxic.

"My mother would yell out, 'Howard, it's the fogger. Get a dozen eggs,' and my dad would run out there with the eggs. They always knew they would get a free dozen eggs; all they had to do was circle the coops and do a really, really good job. The bugs were so bad; my parents were dying to get some relief somehow."

Sometimes, disease would wipe out an entire coop. Barry said his dad solved the problem by not allowing anyone outside the family to enter the coops. "If a farmer came from a diseased farm to see how your chicks were doing, he would carry the disease on his shoes," Howard explained. "That's why I didn't let anyone in the coops, not even people from the Agriculture Department, because they were on farms with problems.

"If the chickens became sick, there was a poultry center in Vineland run by the government that could help. If you had a problem, you could bring it into the Vineland laboratory for a fee and they would recommend the amount of antibiotics to be mixed into the grain mash. The feed company also had a specialist, and the specialist would diagnose and write a prescription. The company had its own facilities for mixing whatever medicine you needed into the chicken feed since you were buying the feed from it by the tons."

Barry was still having nightmares. One night, as he headed up the stairs to brush his teeth, he saw the shadowy silhouette of a rifle on the wall. He held his breath and squeezed his eyes shut. When he opened them, it was gone. Sometimes, he lay in bed and listened to his parents argue. "They would fight and get so angry, and I was scared, so I would go downstairs and beg them to stop.

"Because I was an only child, my parents were almost like my best friends," Barry said. "When I got into fifth or sixth grade—I was around 12 years old—my dad finally leveled with me and told me that the stories the kids in school had told me were true."

Nineteen years earlier, on Monday, March 30, 1953, two shots from a Marlin .22-caliber small-bore action rifle had silenced an argument taking place in the farmhouse kitchen. The bodies of a man and a woman lay on the floor as the blood formed a large, dark pool around them. The man's sons—Norman, age 17, and Sigurd, 16—told police that the argument had started around 12:45 AM. The boys had been listening to the conflict from their bedroom upstairs. Signe Sand, their stepmother, died instantly; Osmund Sand then turned the gun on himself. He died 6 days later at the Atlantic City Hospital without ever regaining consciousness.

The Sands' bodies were found by their 9-year-old daughter, Arlene, at 8:45 that tragic morning. Initially, it was believed to have been a murder-suicide pact because the couple left a series of notes, along with $134 divided up in containers for each of the children. The Sands had been having financial difficulties; Osmund, who had recently sold his 1,200 chickens, had been staying overnight on and off at the diner he owned on Route 9 in Manalapan.

As police investigated, new stories surfaced as to what had really happened on the Sands' farm that early March morning. There was speculation that the boys, who took care of the family's egg and poultry route, did not like their stepmother and did not turn in all the money to her at the end of each day. They kept some for themselves and used it to get into trouble. Even though it was the boys who were stealing the money, Osmund blamed Signe for the shortage, starting that fatal argument. The boys admitted their role in the tragedy, and the judge ruled that they were not allowed to benefit from the sale of the farm.

The money paid for the house at auction first went to pay off any debt associated with the house, and the little money remaining went to Arlene. Along with gaining clear title to the property through the auction, Howard was awarded possession of the court transcripts of the murder-suicide. He told the judge, "I don't want it. I am starting out fresh here, and I don't want to bring bad vibes into it. As far as I am concerned, it is a nothing issue." He refused to take the court paperwork on the crime.

Howard showed Barry the wall where he fixed up the sheetrock that the bullets had torn into. "When my mother arrived there for the first time and saw the damage and the bloodstains, she insisted they put the place up for sale. She hated the place, it was away from her family, it was buggy, and of course there was the crime that had taken place there. My dad saw only the realization of a longtime dream. He told her, 'That's the past; we are going to fix this up and make a new home.' And when they sold the farm years later, my mother was crying. She had grown to love the place and didn't want to leave it.

"Today, when I come home from my secular job in Atlantic City, I look at all the old houses that we used to deliver to. My dad and my late mother said there was a time we must have sold eggs to every home there.

"That farm—even though I loved it as a child—I was afraid of it; there was always an evil presence. I know my parents loved each other, but it wasn't until after they sold and moved out of there that the violent arguments stopped. I always believed there was evil there that was trying to stop us. I feel it was by the grace of God that I was able to survive the farm and grow up and be here today."

That grace brought Barry to the role he holds today, as pastor of the Warren Grove United Methodist Church. He sees God's divine intervention, as he calls it, in other ways. "My wife, Iris Lopez Steinmetz, comes from Puerto Rico," he told me. "Her dad came here first to America. Then he brought his family—Iris, her mother, and her brothers—to work on the cranberry bogs. It was called Simm Place. Her mother was the cook, and the owners of Simm Place had migrant farmers who would come in and pick the cranberries. Iris helped her mother do the cooking for the camp of migrant workers here in Warren Grove. The owners gave the Lopez family a place to live while they were handling the caretaking of the house and property for the owners until the military bought out the cranberry bogs."

Remember those 500 acres that were supposed to be traded to Barry's grandfather? Those were the same bogs that Iris's family took care of.

Iris and Barry met at the Methodist church in Manahawkin, and when Barry felt called by God, he entered the candidacy program and became a pastor. The church that Barry pastors along with Iris sits alongside the former Simm Place property!

The church holds a special service for hunters just before deer season opens, something that Barry says is unique to the Pines. "We give prayers for the hunters and have a reading from the Bible that has something to do with hunting. Over the years, the gunning clubs have heard about it and will come here. It's a unique situation—you see people in camouflage clothes, and you smell beer and cigarettes on them. For some of these hunters, it will be the only time of the year that they set foot inside a church. Accidents can happen in the woods, and I think it makes them feel a little safer coming here first.

"My dad used to shoot deer, among the other animals he killed. I love animals, and I used to try to persuade him not to shoot the deer; I would make noises and do all sorts of things to scare them off. But

I've learned to respect life and death and what people do. Even though it might not be your beliefs, you need to respect that."

Barry's life has come full circle in other ways as well. As part of his ministry, he is a chaplain at the Sea Crest Nursing Home, right behind where his parents' farm used to be and where he used to walk Donny in the woods to collect bottles.

Stewards of the Land

The mist is gently rising off the bogs as the sun begins to climb. It is early October, and the men are preparing for a full day's work. They pull shiny black, chest-high waders over their pants, elastic suspenders crisscrossing their T-shirts. The waders are waterproof one-piece apparel with booted footwear attached to the bottom. It is only 45 degrees on this cool Indian summer morn, but their laborious work will keep them warm, so there is no need to put on anything heavier.

They pile into a truck and head across the farm, passing flooded bogs to be harvested another day. The water reflects the cloudless azure sky as the mist clears from its surface. The men drive along the dams to the cranberry bog they will be working this morning. The bog is roughly 3 acres in size; cranberry bogs in the Chatsworth area range from an acre to roughly 11.5 acres.

Yesterday, the berries were knocked off the plants in this bog with a cranberry harvester, and this morning they are bobbing around at the surface. A cranberry contains four air chambers, causing it to float once it is detached from the vine.

The cranberry harvester is jokingly referred to as an "egg-beater machine" by those outside the cranberry industry because of its appearance; its swirling blades gently knock the berries off the vines as it moves through the water. One man walks in front of the harvester to guide the driver; the vines are trained to grow in certain directions to minimize damage from the machine as it passes over them.

The men work in a synchronized rhythm; they have been harvesting these bogs for several seasons, and each knows his role. Two men guide the yellow inflatable *cran-boom* as a tractor pulls it from the dam. Its purpose is to corral the floating cranberries so they can be drawn up easily into the cranberry cleaner. Another man walks along the edge of the dam, using a blower to push the cranberries off the edge of the bog and inside the cran-boom's floating walls.

Once the berries are safely within the protective walls, the cleaner will begin drawing them up with what looks like a large vacuum hose. The hose will take up both water and berries at the rate of 60,000 pounds per hour.

Operations have just begun at the Sooy family bogs as Andrew and I drive across the dam. Slinging our cameras over our shoulders, we approach the cleaner, now in full swing. Stephen Lee III, who goes by Steve, beckons us to join him on top of the machine so we can get a better view of the process.

The machine vibrates loudly as the berries move up the blue hose. The hose is translucent, and I watch the berries race up the tube as the water splashes around them. With a keen ability to "feel" the machinery, much as he did as a pilot for the U.S. Air Force, Steve monitors the cleaner. He watches the mix of fruit and water move through the tube and get drawn into the cleaner we are standing on.

As the berries and water rise through the center of the machine, they move over a grate that drains the water and pumps it into a truck for return to the bogs. The berries then pass under powerful jets of water that spray away leaves and debris, which are caught and eventually deposited in compost piles at the back of the farm. Nothing goes to waste during the harvesting process.

The cleansed berries make their way up a conveyor belt and into a waiting truck. Besides monitoring the mix of berries and water and listening for clogs, Steve keeps watch on the conveyor and shifts it to ensure a level load. Steve's son, Stephen Lee IV, moves each full truck and then drives the next one into position. Each truck holds 300 barrels of cranberries, equivalent to 30,000 pounds of fruit.

The full trucks head up to the Ocean Spray Fruit Receiving Station a few miles north on Route 563 in Chatsworth. Ocean Spray is a grower-owned marketing cooperative formed in 1930 by three cranberry growers from Massachusetts and New Jersey. Today, it consists of more than 650 cranberry growers from Massachusetts, Wisconsin, New Jersey, Oregon, Washington, and British Columbia and other parts of Canada, as well as about 50 Florida grapefruit growers who joined the cooperative in 1976. The cooperative enables the owners to function as a unit and exchange ideas.

Six generations of Lees have harvested the bogs in Speedwell. The farmers in the area try to sequence their harvests so that they can share equipment. Today, Steve Lee and his son are helping the Sooys harvest their bogs.

Steve points out the different aspects of the process to us as the men rake the fruit into the center of the cran-boom's circle. As the cranberries disappear up the hose, a reel takes up the excess length of cran-boom, and the circle tightens. The men, several feet from the machine we are standing on, are wading in about 2 feet of water.

I'm tempted to grab a pair of waders and head out to watch the process up close. When I vocalize this thought, Steve shares a story with me. Last year, a family friend stopped by the bogs to witness the harvest. He was wearing old clothes and a baseball cap. He stood along the dam, watching the men work. At one point, his curiosity overtook him, and he headed out to where the men were standing in the thigh-high water. Steve turned away, momentarily distracted by a clog in the machine; when he looked back, all he saw was a baseball cap floating on the water.

What his friend did not realize is that although the area where the vines grow is only about 3 to 4 feet deep, the vines are surrounded by a ditch that can be 8 to 10 feet deep. The ditch allows the farmers to flood and drain the bogs. Each bog contains a ramp that allows the machinery and the men to cross the ditch safely.

If you are unaware of how bogs are constructed, you might assume a flooded bog is only a few feet deep, and both father and son had stories to tell of people who literally "got in over their heads." While visitors are generally welcome to view the harvest, it's advisable for them to remain on the dam and follow the instructions of the farmer, who is concerned for both their safety and that of the crew.

With this gentle warning, Steve turns his attention back to the cleaner. As the berries tumble onto the grate, he tells us how his great-great-grandfather—an engineer—came over from Ireland and started the farm in 1868. "He noticed that cranberries grew naturally along the streams, and he found that if you put a dam across the stream and flooded the area, you could protect the cranberries from freezing and get a crop each year. So he began a system of building the bogs. Some of the bogs have been renovated only once in 130 years, which is pretty amazing.

"My great-grandfather had six children, but he died at a young age. His widow couldn't run the farm by herself and raise six children, so she moved back to Philadelphia. The farm had its ups and downs until 1946, when my father and his brother came home from World War II, renovated everything, and started over again."

By now, the bog is almost drained of cranberries, and Steve excuses himself to help the crew clean out the rest of the berries and prepare for the next bog. Andrew and I thank the men for their time and head out, agreeing that the next time we eat cranberries, we'll have a deeper appreciation of the process that gets them to the table.

***

Later in the year, during the less hectic winter season, I caught up with Steve's son, Stephen, who gladly picked up the story where his dad had left off.

"In 1946, my grandfather and my uncle John made a decision to come back to the farm full time; my grandfather had been working at Madden's Hardware in Mt. Holly, which was owned by my aunt Mary. He had the option of going into the hardware business as my uncle Charlie had just passed on. So my grandfather was running my aunt's store.

"He made the decision to come back to the farm and got a loan from Ocean Spray. The Burlington County agricultural agent at the time came into the hardware store when he found out my grandfather wanted to grow cranberries. The agent said my grandfather was a damned fool if he thought he was going to grow cranberries there; the agent thought my grandfather was out of his mind. You probably would have thought the same thing if you had seen how overgrown the farm was. None of the bogs looked the way they do today; it looked like the woods back here."

Stephen showed me a black-and-white photo from those early years, and I could understand the agent's point. Yet this story contains a thread that has run through the stories of all the people I've talked to out here: It's all about having a vision—usually involving goals most people can't appreciate—and the determination to make that vision a reality. In Stephen's grandfather's case, the vision quite literally bore fruit.

Stephen continued, "After a few years, my uncle John made a decision to leave the business, and it was just my grandfather and grandmother. My grandfather pretty much built the farm on his own. But because he was part of Ocean Spray, he was able to benefit from its advice on which direction to go with building the farm.

"Being part of the cooperative is very beneficial because we are a farmers' cooperative that happens to also be in the juice business. It's a pretty good situation as far as being a cranberry grower—not only from the standpoint of being able to share information on the cultural part, but primarily from the business part, where we have a guaranteed home for our fruit. We don't have to worry where we are going to sell it or who's going to buy it. We are able to focus on growing the cranberries, and we have the professional team we hired that focuses on growing the brand and our business for us."

According to Stephen, "Ocean Spray is North America's leading producer of canned and bottled juices and juice drinks and has been the best-selling brand name in the canned and bottled juice category since 1981. Ocean Spray posted fiscal 2007 sales of roughly $1.6 billion."

The cranberry is one of three indigenous fruits in North America, the other two being the blueberry and the Concord grape. Because the cranberry and the blueberry are well adapted to both sandy soil and swampy conditions, they have been a dependable source of income here, even as other Pine Barrens industries rose and fell.

At the time Europeans began to arrive in the New World, Native Americans had long been using the cranberry for medicinal purposes and as a dye. To the early Dutch and German settlers, the white blossom of the cranberry suggested the head of a crane, and they named the fruit *crane-berries.*

James Lind, a physician on the HMS *Salisbury*, which sailed from England to the Plymouth Colony in 1747, experimented with the diets of sailors to find a cure for scurvy, known as the *plague of the sea* because of the numbers of sailors who succumbed to it during long oceanic trips. Lind noted that crewmen who ate citrus fruit recovered quickly. Because cranberries are both high in vitamin C and less perishable than citrus fruits such as lemons or limes, they soon became the favored fruit for those sailing the high seas.

Besides preventing scurvy, cranberries offer a host of other health benefits. Ocean Spray has highlighted the benefits documented in several scientific reports:

> According to the American Heart Association, cardiovascular disease remains the number one health threat affecting men and women in the United States today. Now, a recent review of scientific research suggests cranberries may offer a natural defense against the development of this dangerous disease. Researchers feel that many of these results are due to the fact that cranberries contain a greater concentration of antioxidants than other commonly consumed fruit and that these nutrients may be working together to offer even greater benefits.
>
> The report conducted at Tufts University, and published in *Nutrition Reviews*, found that cranberries offered a range of different benefits that work to promote cardiovascular health. These benefits include effects on cholesterol as well as on blood pressure and the development of blood clots, all established risk factors for heart disease. ...
>
> In fact, one such study revealed that a daily serving of Light Cranberry Juice Cocktail provided an effect that was similar to what has been reported for red wine, a beverage

that has been well publicized for having a positive effect on cardiovascular health.

In addition to an increase in HDL, another study highlighted in the review reported that cranberry [*sic*] lowered the "bad" LDL cholesterol when consumed in increasing amounts over a period of weeks. Cranberry has also been found to inhibit the oxidation of LDL cholesterol, an effect that has been shown to further reduce the risk for cardiovascular disease. Experimental evidence also suggests cranberries may act to reduce the formation of blood clots as well as blood pressure, actions known to lower the risk of stroke.[1]

Cranberries have long been known to ward off urinary tract infections (UTIs) due to unique compounds in the fruit called proanthocyanidins, or PACS. PACS offer an anti-adhesion mechanism that prevents harmful *E. coli* bacteria from adhering to the urinary tract wall. ... According to the National Kidney Foundation, one in five women will develop a urinary tract infection ... during her lifetime, and 20 percent of those will have UTIs on a recurrent basis. The good news is that cranberry research supports not only the reduction of recurrent UTIs by half, but now a new study suggests cranberry compounds may help prevent recurrent UTIs for as long as two years.[2]

Recent findings published in the *Journal of Antimicrobial Chemotherapy* reveal that the cranberry may be the next new weapon in the fight for good oral health. Researchers have discovered that natural compounds in cranberries may help ward off periodontitis, or severe gum disease, by serving as a powerful anti-inflammatory agent. This anti-inflammatory effect may be attributed to unique compounds in the fruit that prevent *P.gingivalis* bacteria from adhering to the teeth below the gum line. This new research offers great promise for the estimated 67 million Americans affected by periodontitis, the primary cause of tooth loss in adults.[3]

Growing these *wonderberries*, as they have been called, requires constant attention. When I asked Stephen to tell me what it's like to be a cranberry farmer, he happily obliged. "It's truly a year-round operation," he said, explaining how the bogs are flooded in the wintertime to protect the buds that will produce next year's crop.

"We will drain the bogs around April 15, and then the bud begins to develop the fruit for that October. During the winter, we will keep a constant flow of water through the bogs so the oxygen level won't deplete—that's first and foremost. We will also put an inch layer of sand on top of the bogs to help the vines grow, sort of like mulching your garden. We don't sand every year, only every couple of years.

"We'll also modify and repair some equipment to get it ready for the season. When spring comes, we kick into high gear. You are literally babysitting the farm constantly—we have someone here all the time from the first part of April until November.

"Once we get the water off the vines, the bud is beginning to break and develop. There are still some cold nights where the temperature can drop into the low 30s, and that bud on the end of the vine will freeze. If it's a hard enough frost, it won't kill the plant, but you will lose the bud, and if you do, you're done. There's no turning back. Cranberries are harvested only once a year. It takes them from April to October to grow. You don't replant them; this is a one-shot deal, so it's vital that we pay attention to the development of the fruit."

Stephen explained that if frost is suspected, the Lees will turn on their irrigation system in the bogs to sprinkle water over the tops of the vines to prevent them from freezing. Before they put in this system, they were producing 50 to 60 barrels per acre. Today, they produce between 250 and 500 barrels per acre. Each barrel holds about 100 pounds of cranberries.

"So on a typical night from about the middle of April through June 15, you are paying very close attention to the Weather Channel, to the dew point, to the forecast, to the cloud cover, to the temperature. In addition to that, you have to make sure your equipment is up and running. And that's just the nighttime.

"During the day, you are primarily focused on getting your fertilizer on, and you begin your Integrated Pest Management (IPM) program. You look at the sky to see if there is any smoke; one part of our job as stewards of the land is to pay attention to what's going on around us. For fire prevention, we clear fire lanes throughout the property."

The IPM program involves sweeping the bog with nets and then analyzing conditions to make a determination about spraying. Before IPM, spraying was done routinely three times a year based on the calendar, not on the conditions. Today's farmers take a more accurate and appropriate response to boost yields while being more protective of the land.

"You are not going to find a better conservationist or environmentalist than a farmer, especially here," Stephen insisted. "The water quality is important, the soil quality is important, the land quality is important. This has been our livelihood for six generations; there is no question about us preserving it."

He continued with the farmers' duties of the late spring. "Once you get to the point where the flowers bloom, we will bring the honeybees in. We contract with a beekeeper to pollinate the cranberries; as they develop, they go from a little white flower to 'out of bloom' during late spring and early summer. We fertilize at various growth stages.

"Then, when it gets to mid-July and it's 95 degrees in the shade, we turn the pumps on again or the fruit will scald and shrivel up. That's not how we make Craisins," he joked, referring to another Ocean Spray success story. The marketing team of the cooperative is constantly looking for innovative ways to grow the brand. It introduced Craisins, a sweetened cranberry snack, in 1993. Today, Craisins come in original cranberry or cherry and orange flavors.

"As we get ready for harvest, we have to watch out for the cold nights again," Stephen said. "That helps them ripen; they can withstand some cold temperatures, but not too cold. Late Indian summer, we continue to watch for forest fires.

"How is the water level in the reservoirs—has it been dry this year? Water is very, very important for us. We need it for protection; we need it for harvest. We recycle the water, and it will get reused. We'll 'borrow' water from the west branch of the Wading River and run it through all the bogs and into the Haines bogs, and from there it will eventually go back into the Mullica River and then the Atlantic.

"In between paying attention to the weather, we are also looking to increase the production of the bogs. We are in the process of renovating about 14 acres that my grandfather put in back in the 1950s, trying to increase our yields, running a business, paying our bills and taxes, and going to meetings. As farmers, my family thinks it's important to contribute from the civic side.

"My dad, uncle, grandfather, and I have all served on boards during our careers. My grandfather was the state board of agriculture president for some time, and my uncle was the vice chair. I currently serve on the county board of agriculture, I'm the vice chair of the town planning board, and I was on the school board down in Green Bank. My dad is on the board of directors for Ocean Spray, he serves on the [New Jersey] Pinelands Commission, and he served as a chair on his church's building committee. My uncle is on the First Pioneer Farm Credit Board, as were my father and my grandfather. Quite frankly, I think it's important for farmers to have an active participation in the political arena, to do that as much as they can—to go to their town meetings to have an understanding about what is going on politically and to give back to the community."

Speaking with Stephen, one gets the impression that he was born in the bogs and intends to die here. "Once it gets into your blood, it never gets out," he said, noting that for many families, life on the farm is the only life they will ever know. "It's unfortunate," he laments, "but in some farm families, the sons or daughters are forced to go into the business: 'This is what I did, this is what your grandfather did, this is what your great-grandfather did, and this is what you are going to do.'"

However, Stephen's passion for this land is more than heredity. It was his choice to come back and pass the legacy on to his sons, Andrew and Patrick.

"With us, it was 'There's the road, here's your bag, go do something else'—and not in a bad way, but more to get a learning opportunity off the farm, which I was able to do. My grandfather specifically recommended doing that, and his reasoning was that in order for you to truly appreciate your own business, your own operation, you have to go out into the real world. You have to learn how things work outside the farm to gain a true appreciation for working for yourself. You have to understand what it is like to have employees, how to treat employees, and what it is like to be an employee and punch a time clock, and so I did that.

"I got two degrees, neither of them involved with growing cranberries at all—they're business degrees. I graduated from the county college in Pemberton with a degree in hospitality management, then transferred to Widener University, just outside Philadelphia, and got a degree in hotel restaurant management in 1993. I worked in the industry from about 1988 to 1999, just a little more than 10 years.

"It's the hotel business, but there's a business side to that—I worked primarily in food and beverage; I ran restaurants and room service, ran a café, couple of different things, so I had a business background coming in here."

Stephen explained that he and his wife, Monica, had dinner with his parents one night, and his dad told him that if this was a good time to leave the hotel business, he was welcome to come home. "But he also made it clear," Stephen emphasized, "that if I wanted to do that, it's great, but if not, that's fine, too. Growing up, I never felt there was any requirement to do this.

"My wife and I made a decision to move back here. We left our apartment in Mt. Laurel, moved home, I quit my job in Philadelphia, and started cranberries—all within 2 weeks! For her, it was culture shock coming here because she's from southeastern Ohio—she grew up in a little town with a grocery store, banks, gas stations, and a couple of schools, and we don't have any of that in Speedwell. Here, the closest grocery store is a half-hour away. I also got used to having stuff right around the corner, but I'm really glad to be doing this—to be the sixth generation of Lees growing cranberries here in Speedwell. Those are certainly big shoes to fill.

"My dad, my grandfather, and my uncle have always strived to be as efficient as possible. When we got to a point when we were making money doing this back in the early years, instead of buying a yacht or a house on the shore or trips to Hawaii or wherever, they smartly put money back into the operation. They are constantly trying to improve it—in the wintertime, that's the time to repair equipment, to say, 'How are we going to do this differently? What are we going to do this year?' Once you get to the point of getting water off the bogs—the growing season goes from April 15 until roughly October—you've got to be ready to go."

Stephen isn't the only sixth-generation Lee to feel cranberry juice coursing through his veins. "My sisters and I grew up helping out during the cranberry harvest and still do that today. I have two younger sisters: Patricia lives here and works up in Mt. Laurel. She has two children, and they come down and help out during the fall. My other sister, Jennifer, lives in St. Louis with her husband, but she comes and takes a week's vacation during the fall to help out also, so we have all been pretty fortunate to be here, doing this."

Cranberries aren't the only crop the Lee family has been involved in. For a while, they also grew blueberries, but they were not as profitable per yield, Steve told me that day in the bogs. Today, the Lees produce a more unusual crop, at least from the standpoint of what most people consider a crop. They grow trees.

Stephen explains. "We began a forestry project by enlisting the help of a forester by the name of Bob Williams down in Glassboro. We had to have the plan approved by the Pinelands Commission. We clear-cut the existing scrub pine trees and did a replanting. If you look at the classical history of a forest, it has to have some sort of event to encourage new growth.

"We've done the forestry project to increase the uses of the land for the next generation; we're improving the life of the forest by what we've done, and there's scientific data to back that up. It was amazing to see the changes in the forest after the trees were cut. We have a plethora of red-headed woodpeckers, which you normally don't see, some bald eagles on the property, and we see red-tailed hawks on a regular basis. We're looking at what's best from a farmer's perspective for the life of the crop; in this case, we're trying to grow trees. We were very active in prepping the land to the extent that we were nationally recognized."

The Lees own just under 2,000 acres of land: 127 acres of cranberries, about 600 acres in planned forest, and the remainder in reservoirs, upland forest, and woodlands. Bob Lees (no relation), who lives up the road in Tabernacle, told me that he never had a job in his life. "If you enjoy what you do, it's not a job," he said. It is readily apparent that

Stephen shares that sentiment. Before I left, he shared a final story with me.

"I had dinner with a college roommate last night, and we were talking. He said, 'It's funny how you look back at different parts of your life, and you think, Oh man, I wish I was doing that, I wish I was doing this. I truly envy what you are doing—your family has created a legacy, you're continuing that legacy, you're raising your family in that legacy, and it's admirable because it's not an easy thing to do.'"

Stephen concurred with his friend. "It truly isn't easy, but it's a privilege to be doing this. This is a 24-hour-a-day, 365-day-a-year operation. You've got to be constantly paying attention, regardless of whether you are in the growing season or not. If you're not looking at the temperature to see how hot it is or whether you have to turn the water on, you're paying attention to a forest fire threat. I don't think people truly understand what it's like to be a steward of the land.

"Unless you have been out here for a good period of time, you can never fully understand what it's like. People think we're out here in the middle of nowhere, but as far as I am concerned, this is God's country. We are blessed and fortunate, and I'm proud to be part of it."

Endnotes

1. Ocean Spray Cranberries, Inc., "Review Finds Cranberries Support a Healthy Heart," press release, January 31, 2008, www.oceanspray.com/news/pr/pressrelease118.aspx (accessed January 5, 2009).

2. Ocean Spray Cranberries, Inc., "Cranberries Provide Urinary Tract Protection for Up to Two Years," press release, August 13, 2007, www.oceanspray.com/news/pr/pressrelease116.aspx (accessed January 5, 2009).

3. Ocean Spray Cranberries, Inc., "Cranberries May Reduce Inflammation Associated with Severe Gum Disease," press release, July 10, 2006, www.oceanspray.com/news/pr/pressrelease103.aspx (accessed January 5, 2009).

Age of Innocence

Childhood can be a magical time of building fortresses, catching frogs and toads, discovering the woods, and reading in a tree house. For the children of the Pine Barrens, it has long meant ice skating on frozen lakes and drying off next to a bonfire of burning tires or picking blueberries in hot, buggy fields and washing blue stains off bodies in the nearest creek.

Most of the Pineys I spoke with recalled being very poor but not knowing they were poor because everyone around them was in the same condition. Besides, they were too busy doing chores and helping their families to give it too much thought. When the work was done, they headed outdoors with friends who lived close by and made their own fun in the woods.

It wasn't only the woods that were magical. Even local industry offered some excitement and wonder to a wide-eyed child.

Everett Applegate is a Chatsworth native. He grew up on the corner of Main and Second Street, next to Applegate's Market, opened by his father in 1944. Chatsworth is a sleepy town of about 600 people, often referred to as the capital of the Pine Barrens.

It was here that Everett and his brother, Dave, and sister, Norma, came of age. Their father and their Uncle Frank owned and operated the Cedar Sawmill at the end of Wilhelmina Road. It was later sold to Herb Wickward, who let the children play there.

Everett recalled fondly, "Unlike the theme parks of today that merely keep kids amused for a few hours, the cedar mill provided my friends and me with endless opportunities to be creative. We invented games, figured out how the machinery operated, built forts and tree houses, and even risked our lives performing daredevil stunts. I can't imagine life as a child without having a sawmill nearby."[1]

Everett recounted how they would roll a 55-gallon barrel that was open on both ends to the top of the cedar slat pile. "Cedar slats were the outer remnants of cedar logs that had been cut into planks for lumber. The slats were sliced into 2-foot lengths with bark on the top side." These piles typically measured 50 feet high and filled an area about the size of a football field.

The kids would roll the barrel to the top of one of the piles, one of them would squeeze inside, and the others would push the barrel off the top and let it roll down the sloped side. Everett said, "It was a dangerous but thrilling ride. And it held out the exciting possibility of painful splinters, bumps, and bruises if you lost your purchase, got ejected, and tumbled painfully down the side of Slat Mountain to the ground. No theme park ride could compare."

Along with their cousins Chick and June, Everett and Dave also built tunnels and tree houses from the cedar. Everett recalled how they "constructed an elaborate network of underground rooms with interconnecting tunnels in the woods behind the mill. One such tunnel took more than a week to construct. We dug long trenches into the damp sandy ground, connecting the tunnels to the rooms.

"After covering the top of the tunnels with cedar slats and planks from the sawmill, we covered the entire area with sand to hide everything from view. We then fashioned two hidden trap doors for entrances and lined the interior with old horse blankets borrowed from our uncle's barn. With candles and flashlights in hand, we'd descend into our self-excavated tombs to tell scary stories or just merge into our forest world. The musty smell of the damp interior remains in my nostrils to this day."[2]

While the girls often joined the boys in different antics and jaunts through the woods, sometimes a girl just had to relax and, well, be a lady of leisure. Everett's cousins Debbie and Sarah often sunbathed on a CB radio tower that their dad had built near their house. The house, which is bordered by woods on two sides, sits at the end of a short side street, with only a few other homes nearby. As isolated as they were back then, people were very innocent, as Debbie remembers it; the two girls would climb the tower and lie on the top platform "naked as jaybirds, and we thought nothing of it." She added, "We were naïve in a different kind of way."

One day, Debbie saw an army helicopter flying by. It was real low, she said—so low that she could see the open door and the guy in the chopper wearing a white helmet. "Wow, they are flying low," she thought. "They must be on maneuvers." Every day, the helicopter would come back, flying just as close.

At home, the two sisters would often wander the grounds clad only in short T-shirts and underwear. One time, a state police trooper followed Debbie home. He was talking with her in the yard when, without giving a thought to what she was wearing, Sarah came running out. The policeman's jaw dropped open. Debbie said, "That's just my sister—she was worried about me when she saw you here."

After that, the state police started dropping by frequently. The girls didn't think anything of it until weeks later when their dad got angry. "You girls have to stop doing what you are doing."

"What are you talking about?" Debbie asked.

"I have the army with helicopters all the time over my house, I have the state police in my yard," he replied.

"But Dad," Debbie explained, "they are on maneuvers."

"Maneuvers!" he retorted. "They're over here looking at your naked asses!"

Even areas designated for sunbathing could prove hazardous. Earl Ward, who lived in Pemberton for part of his childhood, remembered an abandoned gravel pit that became the local swimming hole. "It was open to the public. There was a raft on one end, and we would swim out to it and sunbathe. Some places were shallow, and others were real deep; kids would jump off, and one fellow broke his collarbone. Another guy jumped off the banks—not realizing how shallow it was—and hit his head and had to be in a brace for a while."

Earl's wife, Lois, used to swim in the Rancocas Creek while growing up in Pemberton. "The water was so dark, it looked like tea. You washed your hair in it, you would drink out of it and swim in it—and the cow did, too. I remember swimming once in the creek, and I looked over and there was a cow in the cove!"

Swimming in the creeks and lakes was a favorite pastime for young and old, especially after a hot day in the blueberry fields. While many like to recall their summers in those hot, dry fields, not all speak fondly of them.

"I used to pick blueberries in my father's field. He told me that when he died, he would leave me the fields," Jeff Brower shared. "I told him I didn't want them—give them to my brother. If he left them to me, I would have burned them all down."

Bob Lees remembered how the farmers would have patience with the kids. "Wherever you worked, there was an opportunity to learn how to do something else. If it was a slow or rainy day, maybe they'd take you into one of the buildings and teach you about pumps or mechanics. You might be only 10 or 11 years old, and they would hand you a wrench and teach you, and that's how you learned things."

Mary Camburn recalled getting paid a nickel a pint for the blueberries she picked. "I thought it would be fun, but it was hot, and I couldn't go to the lake during the day with my friends. My mother offered me money each week if I would clean the house, and I left the blueberry fields in a hurry." She remembered the boys throwing blueberries at the girls and how she would leave the fields with blue-stained skin.

Bob Hagaman, mayor of Weekstown and pastor of Jenkins Chapel in Jenkins Neck, gave up picking blueberries because he got only a penny and a half a pint and ate more than he picked.

Most of the money the children earned picking blueberries went toward their school clothes or supporting the family or into a bank account. Occasionally, they would get to keep some to spend on penny candy or other such luxuries. This thriftiness lasted into their adulthood. Charlie Ashmen told me that he had 35 cents' spending money for a week in Atlantic City as a young man. "The first day, a quarter fell through the boardwalk and I dug for 2 days," he said, laughing.

When the long days of summer ended, it was time to return to school. One-room schoolhouses dotted the Pine Barrens. Today, some of them remain and have been reincarnated as historical societies, such as the one in Lacey Township; there are historically preserved school buildings such as the one in Tabernacle, churches such as the one in Jenkins Neck, and even homes, as in Plumsted Township.

These one-room schoolhouses of the past have many things in common besides the single room that gives them their name. They were heated by potbellied stoves that the teachers would start up early in the morning so that the room would be warm when the school-children arrive. The schools housed several grades at one time, and the memories they evoke in those who attended them don't ever seem to fade.

The late Jack Cervetto, of Warren Grove, described it this way: "In the school room, there were two rows of desks with attached seats for two pupils at each desk. All the time I attended this school, I sat in the same seat, as did the others until they graduated. … There was a pleasing scent caused by blackboard chalk and the smell of oak wood burning that I have lived with all my life. The school is now owned by a deer-hunting club, and I visit in deer-hunting time. Every year when I visit the boys in hunting season, I pick up a chair and place it on the spot where I sat when I attended school there. It is difficult to explain the feeling."[3]

Andrew and I had the pleasure of sitting with four women in the former Lacey one-room schoolhouse, which now harbors the Lacey Township Historical Society, as they shared their memories with us. Historical Society president Eleanor Ditton organized the meeting, and members and friends Mahala Landrum, Virginia Schoenberg, and Mary Camburn turned out. Unfortunately, the newly installed heating system was not working, and perhaps we would have been better served had we coaxed the old potbellied stove back into action. Despite the chilly conditions, these marvelous ladies painted a vivid portrait of golden school days gone by that Andrew and I were honored to hear.

Virginia's father attended college for 1 year at Rider University (known back then as Rider College). "He would take the train from Forked River to Trenton. He attended only 1 year because he won a scholarship for having the biggest rooster. After that year, his father got sick, and they didn't have money to pay for college, so he came home and worked. But he always told me how he went to college on a rooster."

Mary told us how all the kids in her school were "angels." She was so angelic herself that she spent much of her school days behind the potbellied stove. Sometimes kids would toss crayons onto the top of the stove, and as they melted, the stove would smoke. "Some days we would get sent home, and other times we had to sit outside in the yard," she said.

Virginia explained that instead of the parent-teacher associations of today, there were organizations called neighborhood clubs. They furnished cans of Campbell's soup, and sometimes the pupils would throw a can in the stove when the teacher wasn't looking, and it would explode. That guaranteed being sent home.

Mary recalled how the "angels" in her school affected the teachers. "Mrs. Jackson was an exceptionally good teacher until we drove her crazy," she told us. "She doped herself with Bromo-Seltzer constantly and it dulled her mind," Mahala said. "You don't know how much Bromo-Seltzer she drank," Mary added. "If she ran out during the day, she would send someone out to the store to get more." "This is where we got our education," Mahala quipped.

"Mrs. Eno would come in Monday morning and write the week's schedule on the blackboard," Mary explained. "I liked math, so I would do all the math work, and someone else would do all the history, and by the end of the morning, we had the week's work finished. Then we would say it's a nice day for a nature walk. Mrs. Eno loved taking us on nature walks, so off we went. This went on for weeks until sometime after Christmas—the school board must have gotten wind of it. Mrs. Eno was gone; we got Mrs. Paul, and when she said Jump, we said, How high? and she whipped us into shape."

"Mrs. Paul sent the three worst boys out to get a Christmas tree," Virginia said. "Only two came back. She asked where the other boy was, and they said they didn't know; he must have gone on home. When we left the building to go to the bus, we heard this awful noise, and there was the missing boy—tied to the top of the Christmas tree! Mrs. Paul had to go find something to cut him down with."

Bob Hagaman recalled a memorable school day: "There were three of us—my brother and me and a friend of ours, and I was the youngest one. One morning before school, we were making the circuit to check on the traps we set. One of the traps was in an old barn. It was getting late, and I was tired of walking, so I told them, 'I can't go any farther. I'm going to school. You guys are going to be late.' They said, 'Nah, we aren't going to be late,' so I left them and went to school. They didn't show up. About half an hour after school started, they walked in. You should have smelled them—they had caught a skunk in the trap in that barn and got sprayed! They came to school with those clothes on, and the teacher ran out of the place. We had to open all the windows," he said, chuckling.

Some of the boys weren't just mischievous—they were downright rowdy. That's when the police officers had to take over. Bob Lees has worn many hats, from firefighter to carpenter to police officer and many others.

He did not carry a gun. "If we had one, we wouldn't have wanted it. You didn't need it," he told me. "You're not supposed to know what we did, but if a kid was a little rowdy, we'd load him up in the car and take him out somewhere like Carranza Road. We'd bang him up a bit and leave him there and let him find his own way home. I've had these kids come up to me years later as adults and thank me for what I did. They never did anything like that again. It was a different world then, and most kids had respect."

It was a different world in a lot of ways. The children in the Pine Barrens were often sheltered and indifferent to the chaotic world around them. I spoke with people who were unaffected by the Depression, World War II, and the turbulent 1960s, with its race riots, Vietnam War, and make-love-not-war generation. They were concerned with their everyday lives—not with the headlines—and did what was necessary to survive. Life went on as it always had; there was work to be done throughout the changing seasons of the Pines.

As a young man in the 1960s, George Carroll spent a lot of time in the Pines—particularly around Colliers Mills, where he proposed to his wife, Reggie. He soon learned that it wasn't just those living in the Pines who could be blind to the events and realities of the outside world; it was also the case with many inner-city youth.

From his home in a Trenton suburb during those years, George sought to make a difference. Recalling how he had loved to camp in the Pine Barrens as a boy, he approached the Mercer Street Friends Center—a Quaker-run organization—about starting a Boy Scout troop. He recalled that the director, an older Jewish woman with painful memories of the Holocaust, had concerns about seeing young boys dressed in brown uniforms marching around. However, George eventually won her over, and the troop got its start.

"For 3 years, Boy Scout Troop 130 took young men—mainly African-American and later Spanish-speaking—camping in places like Colliers Mills," George told me. "We would hold Boy Scout meetings in our home. In the middle of all the race riots, a van filled with inner-city kids would pull up in front of our door, and the neighbors would look out their windows as the kids spilled out from the van; it was interesting."

George continued, "I would teach them how to build fires, how to camp out. We had good volunteer leaders—one black fellow had come back from Vietnam, and he knew the outdoors from being in the army, and he helped me with the troop.

"These kids didn't have anything, and we did the best we could with them, but it was tough. We would meet with the boys and their mothers and give them a list of what they needed to bring on the camping trip, such as flashlights, pots, pans, and sleeping bags. But they didn't have any of these things. I'd come to the door in the morning and ring the bell to pick the boy up, and he'd be there with a blanket, a jacket, and a peanut butter and jelly sandwich. The kids would call them *choke sandwiches* because you'd choke on them when you ate them, and that's all they had. So we would bring pots and pans and whatever other supplies were needed.

"There was no such thing as tomorrow for them. They didn't know how to take care of anything. Nothing in their life promised a tomorrow. The idea of taking care of something so you would have it for the future was foreign to them. They lived hand to mouth—this is all they knew.

"I think I learned more from them than the other way around. There were certain games I would teach them, and this proved fascinating to me. With the Boy Scouts, you had a regular routine: There would be a lesson, and then you'd play some games, but the games didn't work the way they were designed to work. When you played tag, they *wanted* to be It. These kids were starved for attention, and they actually liked being It. So they reversed the idea of the game, and I had to rethink how to teach and play games with them because they viewed things differently.

"Another thing that amazed me was that they would call me and the other leaders Mr. and our last names, but they would mix them up. Sometimes they would call me by the name of the black leader from Vietnam, or they would call him Mr. Carroll, and they didn't care. They were colorblind to us; all they knew was that we represented authority figures, and that blew my mind. Here we were—a white Catholic guy, a black man who had served in Vietnam, a Quaker organization, a Jewish woman, and these black and Spanish-speaking inner-city kids in the late 1960s. All we wanted to do was make a difference, and we were to these kids."

Sometimes, as George found out, kids can bring a whole new perspective to an adult's eyes. Lucille Bates-Wickward recalled the most wonderful Christmas she ever had, and she shared her memory with me: "We had a cabin up in the woods in Chatsworth that we went to on weekends. On this particular Christmas—probably in the early 1970s—we took the kids out to cut down a tree of their choice. We were in a pickup truck, and we stopped when they saw this tree. It was a pine tree with about six branches on it, and they thought it was the most beautiful tree they ever saw.

"My son got out—he was probably about 13 years old at the time—and he cut it down. They dragged it into our cabin and put it up in a bucket of sand. They decorated it with all homemade decorations. For example, they took pinecones and spray painted them and put glitter on them. We popped corn in the fireplace and strung the popcorn and put it on the tree. We all went out and scooped cranberries, and then they strung the cranberries. They got paper cups and covered them with tinfoil and made bells out of them. Next came the paper chains in red and green.

"It was actually the ugliest tree we had ever gotten. There were no lights on it. But when the kids were finished decorating, it was the most beautiful tree that we ever had. They were so proud of this tree.

"Now I'm sure if I showed you a picture of it, you wouldn't think much of it. I don't think it would have won any awards. There has never been a repeat of that Christmas. But today, when I'm in the diner and I hear people talking about going to different places for Christmas and saying 'Oh, what a beautiful tree you have!' I'm thinking to myself, 'I've seen the most beautiful tree, and there will never be another one like that one.'"

Endnotes

1. Everett Applegate, *Escape From the Pines* (Cassville, NJ: Cloonfad Press, 2006), 99.

2. Ibid., 99–100.

3. Jack Cervetto, *Living With the Pine Barrens* (Toms River, NJ: Ocean County Historical Society, 2000), 3.

Battle at Painted Rock

L ong before I moved to Jersey, I was familiar with the seemingly endless, unbroken stretch of pines lining Route 539. My sister and her husband were the first to relocate here from New York, and our parents discovered an alternate route to their home when the summertime traffic on the Garden State Parkway proved too much. This route passed through Lebanon State Forest, which has since been renamed to honor former New Jersey Governor Brendan Byrne.

I remember the miles quickly becoming a blur as we left Fort Dix and passed through Manchester and into Barnegat. Other than an occasional mile marker, there was virtually nothing to indicate your position along the route should you break down or need to tell someone where to meet you. Journeying southward, I became accustomed to the scraggly forest of pine and underbrush, carpeted with white sugar sand.

On a hot summer day, my eyes would play tricks as puddles of water seemed to appear and then disappear on the roadbed. This "highway mirage" is actually caused by light waves being refracted near the roadbed because of the density of the hot air rising from the surface. As a child, I had to pass numerous such "puddles" before I was convinced that I could not trust what my eyes were telling me.

Finally, when I was ready to doubt any aberration that came along, it appeared: a large painted boulder, tucked in among the pines on the right side of the road. Though I tried to convince myself that it was only an illusion, the bright paint was indisputable. I don't recall the design that was painted on the rock the first time I saw it, but suddenly the trip "down south" wasn't so boring any more.

On subsequent trips, I looked forward to spotting the rock and witnessing its latest transformation. One year it was a bright orange pumpkin with a gaping black mouth and two small teeth; a month later, a large brown turkey, adorned with multi-colored feathers that seemed to protrude from its back, sprawled across the white rock.

Who painted this rock? And why? And how did it get there in the first place? Anyone familiar with the Pine Barrens knows that boulders are definitely not characteristic of the landscape. For me, there was something magical about the appearance of the painted rock after so many miles of uniform forest.

I came to learn that I was not the only traveler who looked forward to the changing of the rock's design. In other areas of the Northeast, travelers could watch the changing of the seasons: tiny green buds sprouting on the trees in the spring; soft, full leaves casting shadows during the summer months; a picturesque canvas of autumn colors in the fall. But here in the Pine Barrens, where the trees stay green all year, unless a fire roars through, we came to rely on the rock to mark the changing seasons.

***

The rock sits on the southbound side of Route 539, almost 6 miles north of the Route 72 intersection. It is located in the Greenwood

Wildlife Management Area, which is part of the Pinelands National Reserve. On February 8, 1979, Governor Brendan Byrne signed Executive Order 71, allowing for the formation of a 15-member Pinelands Commission to oversee the country's first National Reserve.

On June 28, 1979, the legislature supplemented the law with the Pinelands Protection Act, which Byrne immediately signed. The act mandated that local land ordinances and municipal master plans conform to the Comprehensive Management Plan being created by the new commission. This legislation protects more than 1 million acres of pinelands, covering 22 percent of the most densely populated state in the nation.

Route 539, paved in the early 1960s, traverses the eastern flank of the Pine Barrens. It is a popular route for those traveling from Philadelphia or the western part of New Jersey near Trenton or coming off Interstate 195 and making their way to the Jersey Shore—to Long Beach Island (LBI) in particular. During the height of summer, it can take a few red lights before you clear the left turn onto Route 72, which becomes the causeway to LBI.

Today, the painted rock is a fabled landmark alerting travelers that Route 72 is just ahead, but once it was just another rock. It is believed that in the 1960s, a truck carrying rocks to build one of the jetties in Barnegat Light on LBI deposited the rock in its current location. Why it was left there is still a matter of debate. Some say it fell off as the truck headed into the curve of the road; others say the driver dropped it in order to pass a weight inspection.

The rock measures 5 feet in width, stands 4 feet high, and spans 7 feet in length. Some have joked that it started as a pebble and achieved its size from years of painting.

Early on, it became a magnet for vandals, who sprayed it with graffiti. Messages and fraternity letters were often found scrawled across its surface.

Edward Gillesheimer was just one of thousands who regularly passed the rock in his travels. Ed owned Riverside Amusements, a business in Beachwood that painted video games and pinball machines. When he retired, he had a lot of spare paint.

So around 1997, Ed became the mysterious rock artist of the Pine Barrens. Arriving around 7:00 on Monday mornings, he unloaded the paint from a blue Chevy van and wielded his paintbrush. It took him only about 45 minutes to paint most designs, he said, depending on the intricacy. This explains why few people ever saw him at work.

Ed doesn't consider himself an artist, but rather someone who liked the rock and felt it should be more than a random bulletin board. The designs were his own, and most of the themes were seasonal. The first time he painted the rock was just before Easter. He painted a large red tulip and the words "Happy Easter" on the side facing the road, leaving his initials near the bottom of the rock, toward the back. The following Easter, he painted several tulips—yellow ones this time.

Painted Christmas trees complemented the Pines in December, while shamrocks appeared in time for Saint Patrick's Day. Red hearts showed up in February 2001—one was emblazoned with *Fran* in the center, leading some of Ed's friends to suggest that his real motivation was to save money on a Valentine's Day gift for his wife.

Not all Ed's themes were so obvious. In November 2000, the rock was completely white. Was he feeling uninspired that Monday? No, he said, he was just trying to portray a white cat caught in a snowstorm.

When Fran bowled a 204, Ed commemorated her victory with a bright yellow bowling pin and the score all over the rock in varying colors. He shared fond memories of that game with me, but not all his artwork was celebratory. When Millie Aceino, the wife of his best friend, Matty, passed away in 2001, Ed painted a musical scale on the side of the rock and the title of Millie's favorite hymn, "How Great

Thou Art," across the front. Matty passed away in 2005, and Ed misses them both. It was a very sad time in his life.

I asked Ed if he had a favorite design, and without hesitation, he said he was most proud of the maroon background with "Census 2000" in white across the rock's face. "It was the year I did the census," he recalled. "I painted the rock to look like the badges we wore. I called on someone down on LBI, and when he answered the door, he looked at my badge and said he had just passed a rock recently that looked like it." Ed said he'd painted it, and the man promptly invited him to paint a design on the wall in his house. Ed politely declined. "I'm not an artist," he told me. "I just like the rock."

Near the end of his stint with the census, Ed was working out of the bureau's Trenton office when a story by Karen Sudol about the painted rock, titled "Rock Star: Whiting Man Adds Color to Lacey Township Roadside," appeared in *The Press of Atlantic City*.[1] When Ed got into work that morning, not yet aware of the article, his boss announced, "We have a rock star with us today."

Occasionally, the rock star was caught in the act; Ed recalled the time one fan stopped and handed him $50 for paint.

Over the years, expressions of appreciation for Ed's work have come from near and far; they include a Comcast news story about the rock that was broadcast from Maine to Delaware. A vacationer once sent Ed a letter of thanks and enclosed $20, while another admirer left a colorfully painted wooden sign at the site that said simply, "Enjoy your work." Residents of the retirement village of Cedar Glen Lakes, where Ed lives, would stop at the rock on their occasional bus trips to Atlantic City to admire their neighbor's handiwork.

A letter that ran in the *Beach Haven Times* on January 24, 2001, read, in part, as follows:

> For many years I have traveled Route 539 South from Allentown to Manahawkin where we own a condo at

Fawn Lakes. Approximately five to six miles from Route 72 there is a large rock on the side of the road. Many times there was graffiti written over the entire rock—and it was a complete eyesore for travelers to observe. Several years ago, some unknown person, or persons, decided to change the atmosphere and started painting various scenes on the rock—in accordance with the season or holiday at each different painting.

At times, other people have left signs they had painted with statements, i.e., "Good Job," "Well Done," "Thanks," etc. ... So it seems that along with myself and my family and friends who enjoy seeing this work of art, many others seem to be grateful also.

As a former resident of New Jersey, moved to West Virginia in 1977, I plan to try my skill at "rock painting" in the near future. I anxiously await each trip to Manahawkin—especially to see "what's next on the Rock!"[2]

As with so many things in our country, the fate of the rock changed after September 11, 2001. Ed recalled heading out 3 days after the fall of the Twin Towers with gallons of paint in his van and discovering that the rock had already been repainted by someone else. "They did such a good job," he said, "better than I was doing. It was red, white, and blue like the flag and it was really nice, so I left it alone. I haven't painted it since."

The new mystery painter was Jennifer Gilliam, 8 months pregnant with her first child when she painted the rock. Jim Rahn, a former mathematics teacher at Southern Regional High School in Manahawkin, has a section on his website dedicated to the painted rock. Jennifer sent this to Jim: "I painted the flag on it in 2001. I always wondered who was the man painting it before then. I waited a week after 9/11 to see if he would come and paint it. I was wondering if you knew if he is still around and if he liked the flag? I didn't want to stop him from painting any thing else on it, I thought that since it hadn't changed in awhile before 9/11 he was not able to do it. I hope the new painting made him smile."[3]

While Jennifer's work did make Ed smile, not everyone passing the rock shared his sentiments. As the war heated up, someone decided the prominent rock would make a good spot for political statements. Blue, red, and black peace sign symbols replaced the American flag, and the letters *AWS* appeared in 2005.

Soon an indecent graffiti message directed at the *AWS* painters appeared.

The battle angered another Ed—Ed Napinski, a Korean War veteran who had been touching up the rock with red, white, and blue paint after Jennifer first put the flag there. He knew Ed Gillesheimer only as "an old guy who had a van" and thought Gillesheimer had stopped painting the rock because of his age. "Everybody likes the flag," Napinski thought, so by occasionally retouching it, he made sure that the design did not fade.[4]

Napinski was glad that Jennifer had painted the flag because while he didn't mind doing the touch-ups, he felt he was not artistic enough to have done the whole thing. "It takes a certain know-how to paint the stripes and get them straight," he explained.[5]

Napinski told Nicholas Clunn, a reporter for the *Asbury Park Press*, that the people who had painted the peace signs were *lowlifes*. This caused Mary Palmer of Stafford Township to fire off a letter to the newspaper:

> For years, someone painted topical designs on a large roadside rock, commemorating holidays such as Halloween and Christmas. It was a treat for drivers facing a long haul through the monotonous Pine Barrens. We

looked forward to seeing what new design would appear on the rock. Then came the terror attacks of 9/11. An American flag was painted on the rock. I'm sure we all found comfort in it, especially those of us who had friends or relatives affected by the attack, although it was a tragedy for all Americans. It was a time of almost unparalleled unity in our country and a rare time of worldwide support for the United States.

But time passed. There were no more holidays commemorated on the boulder. The flag design remained. I love our flag, but I was sad that no one was changing the design each season. The deaths in Iraq continued as insurgents flooded the country. Americans began to turn against the war, even many of those who had at first supported the war turned against it.

Finally, someone took paintbrush in hand to repaint the boulder, this time with peace symbols. I was overjoyed. I thought maybe, at last, the majority of Americans had had enough. But, more than that, what I love so much about our country is that we are all free to express our thoughts, ideas, and feelings. In the middle of nowhere, on a rock by the side of the road, somebody had used that freedom to have his or her say.

So, let's not go off half-cocked and call these symbols of peace "a disgrace." Let's not call the people who painted the symbols "lowlifes." The rock doesn't belong to any of us in particular. If it belongs to anyone, it belongs to all of us who live around there or pass by. Our nation, too, is not the sole possession of just a few of us: It belongs to all of us—to those, like my relatives, who wore the uniforms and fought the wars, and even to those who protested those wars.[6]

Jennifer Gilliam believed that *AWS* stood for "Anti-War Statement." She and her husband, Air Force Lt. Douglas Gilliam, with their 3-year-old son, Gavin, in tow, repainted the rock with the American flag in early July 2005, a week before Douglas left for a 3-month tour overseas.[7]

A war veteran offered Jennifer money for paint. Passing cars honked their horns, and drivers waved and yelled, "Thanks!" Some offered to get coffee for the Gilliams, who live on McGuire Air Force Base.

The battle has continued to rage as the painted rock has morphed from a jetty-bound boulder to a roadside memorial. In December 2007, I counted more than 30 flags of various sizes surrounding the rock, still adorned with an American flag. Most of the flags bore the stars and stripes, and a few black-and-white POW-MIA flags were mixed in. Some were flown from elaborate poles topped with gold eagles; others were simply anchored to the ground.

As much as Jennifer hopes that the flag that she and Douglas repainted will remain, she recognizes that it is not under her control. "I painted a rock that didn't belong to me," she said. "It's a free country."

Regardless of what people's reactions to the artwork on the rock are, its purpose may have gone beyond aesthetic and political statements. Chuck Solimone, captain of Lacey Township's Emergency Medical Services, said that the rock has helped police and EMTs locate stranded accident victims, as 911 operators sometimes ask them how far they are from the rock. "We use that as a landmark out there," Chuck said. "It's very important to us."[8]

Ed Gillesheimer has no regrets about any of it. He and his twin sister, Gloria, recently celebrated their 80th birthday together. More than 100 people attended. "It's been a great run," he said.

In 2005, Susan Ortiz penned a tribute to the painted rock and its artists; her words appear on Weird New Jersey's website:

Some rocks are big, and some are small.
Some aren't worth a mention at all.
But here is the story of a rock so unique
You'll have to go see it once your curiosity is piqued.

I found it one day when I changed my direction.
It was just sitting there like a big purple confection.
Rocks come in all colors, but there are none that can change
All the colors of the rainbow like this boulder. It's strange.

Red tulips at Easter, green shamrocks for St. Pat.
It was shiny gold at Christmas and once gray as a rat.
It masquerades as a pumpkin at Halloween,
And it changes for everything in between:

A Thanksgiving turkey, Flynn's Christmas tree,
Remembering Millie, and the Florida Keys,
Red for the Census, fireworks, a ghoul,
Hearts, stars, and even a flag or two.

It once had a symbol that couldn't be explained.
Next to infinity. The mystery remained.
Most of the time it's just signed by "ED."
Who he is it has never been said.

I saw "Welcome home Marilyn" on a white envelope
Filled with a handful of dirt and possibly hope.
Two names and a day from 1978:
Could this be the hint of some time travelers' fate?

When "The Boss" came back, the rock celebrated.
With a flag and song titles, it looked so elated.

Someone once posted a very neat sign
Proclaiming it "The Painted Rock of 539."

It's at the side of the road in the Greenwood preserve
Along a Pine Barrens stretch near a wide curve.
I stop and take a picture whenever I go past
Because I don't know how long this tradition will last.

So when you're traveling Route 539 South
Pass mile marker 20 and keep a lookout.
It's past one guardrail and just before the next
Pull into the sand and prepare to be vexed.

And if you're heading north on 539
Six miles past 72 on the left that's where you'll find
The painted rock in all its glory
Telling another colorful story.

But since 9/11 it's been red, white, and blue.
Why it hasn't changed, I think I've a clue.
Look at that rock and you'll know I'm not wrong—
Just like our country it's solid and strong.

Layer upon layer the rock remains coated.
Who is the painter? Who's so devoted?
Who would have known we'd get so involved?[9]

Endnotes

1. Karen Sudol, "Rock Star: Whiting Man Adds Color to Lacey Township Roadside," *The Press of Atlantic City*, June 14, 2000, CI.

2. "Local Rock Artist Carves Out a Fanciful Niche on Route 539" [Letter to the Editor], *Beach Haven Times*, January 24, 2001.

3. Jim Rahn, "Rt 539 Painted Rock," jamesrahn.com, July 1, 2007, james rahn.com/personal/rock.htm (accessed December 29, 2007).

4. Nicholas Clunn, "Painted Boulder Provokes Man's Ire," *Asbury Park Press*, July 4, 2005, BI.

5. Nicholas Clunn, "Rock Becomes Battleground for Passers-by," *Asbury Park Press*, July 17, 2005, AAI.

6. Mary Palmer, "Topic of the Day: Roadside Artwork" [Letter to the Editor], *Asbury Park Press*, July 15, 2005.

7. Clunn, "Rock Becomes Battleground for Passers-by."

8. Ibid.

9. Susan Ortiz, "New Jersey's Most Painted Rock," WeirdNJ.com, 2005, www.weirdnj.com/index.php?option=com_content&task=view&id=37& Itemid=28 (accessed January 14, 2009).

Shooting the Curl

It was a hot, dry May morning in 1992 as Jeff Brower, forest fire warden for Section 5 of Division B of the New Jersey Forest Fire Service, drove his 1990 Dodge Power Ram through Lacey Township. He had just picked up his crewman, Kevin Flynn, and the pair were on their way to check on Tom Brown Jr.

Tom owns a wilderness survival school in Bethlehem, New Jersey. Since 1978, he has taken hundreds of students into the Pine Barrens and taught them how to track animals, observe nature, and survive in the wilderness. He was camping off Switch Road in the Pine Barrens with several students as Jeff approached.

Jeff reminded Tom that because of the extremely dry conditions, he needed to run a *cold camp*, meaning no campfires. The two were chatting amicably when a call came in from the Cedar Bridge fire tower on Route 539, reporting that smoke had been spotted. Jeff asked where. "Tuckerton railroad bed" was the response.

"Man, we're close," Jeff said to Kevin. The abandoned rail bed was only about 3 miles up the road from where the men were standing.

Jeff advised Tom to pack up camp and jumped into his rig, with Kevin climbing into the well in the back. As they headed off toward the fire, Jeff's hopeful thought was that this probably wasn't going to be much, despite the wind that had begun to kick up.

As he approached the railroad bed just before 11 AM, Jeff saw that the fire was starting to *walk the dog*—a term used to describe fast-moving, wind-driven fires. He drove down a little dirt road toward the fire, which was racing hard in their direction. The blaze had already gotten a good bite on the woods and was starting to take off. It sounded like a freight train roaring through the pines.

Jeff stopped the truck and yelled to Kevin to throw him a backfire torch. As he grabbed the torch, the fire roared through the canopy and over the two men. "We got to get the hell outta here!" Jeff yelled as he jumped back into the truck.

As he drove back toward the rail bed, the division office called. Tom Tansley, assistant division warden, asked Jeff what he needed. "I need the world," he said. "She's taking off; she's going to be a maker."

At that point, the fire was moving parallel to the rail bed and heading toward the Garden State Parkway. "Kevin, we've got to get in front," Jeff yelled. He grabbed the radio and called his best friend and fellow firefighter, Jeffrey Ryan. "Jeffrey, where are you?" he shouted. "You got to get here real quick—the Tuckerton railroad bed—and bring whoever else you have."

There were power lines close to the Garden State Parkway. Jeff headed for them. Other engines were screaming to the scene by this time, and the Forest Fire Service's observation helicopter, a Jet-Bell Ranger manned by state fire warden David B. Harrison, was hovering overhead. Jeff asked for an update and was told the fire was headed toward him.

"Give me the torch," he barked to Kevin. By then, the fire had reached the power lines. As Kevin tried to hand him the torch, the fire jumped over them again and raced across the four lanes of the

Parkway. Normally, a road will stop or slow a fire, but this blaze was raging out of control.

The two men climbed back into the vehicle and bounced over the woods and onto the southbound lane of the Parkway. A state trooper was standing alongside the highway. "What do you need?" he asked.

"Stop this goddamn road—shut it down now!" Jeff yelled as he tore through the trees on the median, crossed the northbound lanes, and headed into a low-lying area. Jimmy Roy, riding on truck #B27, came in behind him. "The smoke was so thick you couldn't see nothing. I was driving and went whoosh, right into a little pond," Jeff recalled. He called for Jimmy, who got his winch cable out, hooked it to Jeff's truck, and pulled him out.

The head fire was beginning to hiss. It sucked up burning embers and deposited them on dry timber, igniting more blazes as its destructive momentum continued.

The radios crackled as the men of Division B exchanged position data and updates on the blaze. Jeff knew he was in trouble. He couldn't see anything, and the fire was tearing up the ground all around him. "That's when I called Dave and said, 'Can you get me out of here?'" The radios suddenly fell silent. Some of their own were in trouble, and all channels were kept clear so the two men could communicate.

"Yup," Dave replied calmly from the chopper. He eyed Jeff's tenuous position on the ground. "But you got to shoot the curl. When I see the nose of your truck, I'll tell you to turn right."

"I said 'OK' and told Jimmy, 'You stick right on my ass, we are getting out of here.' I told Kevin—he was in the back of the truck in the well—'You lay down and suck diamond plate, I don't want to see you.'"

"I got to start the pump," Kevin cried as he turned it on.

Jeff shut it off. "The pump quit," Kevin said.

"You ain't going to squirt no water," Jeff commanded. "Just lay down and suck diamond plate!"

Jeff drove on. "When Dave said 'Now!' I turned right," he recalled.

"You're out!" Dave yelled, and a sense of relief washed over the men. Jeff turned onto the road behind the Oyster Creek nuclear plant and headed back toward the fire's flank to help the other firefighters control the blaze. It was 4 days before he slept, and 7 before he saw home.

"Being a section warden is not a job," Jeff said to me. "It's a way of life."

At 6-foot-5, Jeff towered over many of the men in Division B. Today, instead of a shiny red fire truck, he motors around in a golf cart because of the effects of multiple sclerosis. In 1998, when he was no longer able to meet the physical requirements of the department, he was forced to retire.

While Jeff may be dependent on a walker and golf cart today, he stands taller and prouder than most people I know. His courage and dedication to the Forest Fire Service make him a giant in the eyes of those around him. As a boss, he wasn't always well-liked by those who had to answer to him, but today he is loved by the guys who knew he would always bring them out alive.

"I had a reputation," Jeff shared with me. "I would never leave any of my men behind. If my men were still in a fire, I went in to get them. That's one thing that I am proud of. The men would say, 'Go with Jeff. He'll get you hot, but he'll bring you out alive.'"

Jeff is a fourth-generation Piney and proud of it. "You can't call yourself a Piney until you are fourth generation," he informed me. "Our family goes back to the early 1800s here in Chatsworth."

As a young man, Jeff participated in all the seasonal labors of the Pines—pine balling in the spring, picking blueberries and huckleberries in the summer, scooping cranberries and gathering moss in the fall, and hunting and trapping throughout the winter. But as early as the second grade, he knew he wanted to work for the fire service when he grew up, just like his father, his uncle, and other family members.

At 14, Jeff was allowed to help out only by filling the torches with gas and assisting with the portable pumps. By the time he was 18, he was climbing aboard the "shiny red trucks" he had dreamed about as a child, under the watchful eye of now retired former section warden Bill Sloan.

Jeff majored in forestry at Paul Smith College on the shores of Lower St. Regis Lake in upstate New York. "I remember the very first movie they showed us when I got there. I was sitting in the auditorium with 500 kids, and I hear 'Lanoka Harbor, B2.' I traveled 520 miles to hear my old boss [Bill Sloan] on the screen."

Jeff's aggressiveness helped him move up the ranks quickly. Starting as a crewman, he was quickly promoted to airdrop dispatcher and then served as a forest fire observer in the towers, working at Batsto and Apple Pie Hill and ending up at the Lebanon fire tower. He advanced to forest fire control technician, became section fire warden, and retired as an assistant division warden.

"I could have gone further, but I kept turning down promotions," Jeff said. "Hindsight is 20/20—I could have gotten more in my pension, but money isn't everything. It's not what I wanted, really. I told the state fire warden when he wanted to make me a division warden and then an assistant state fire warden, I'll take the promotion if I can have my truck back. He said my truck riding days were over, so I told him I didn't want it.

"I wanted to go back and be with my men. I missed that—there's nothing better. My men all took care of me like you wouldn't believe, like they were my own family." Jeff told me that rarely did any of the men share their fire stories outside the department, so I was honored that he was willing to tell them to me. "We didn't want our families to worry and know how bad things got sometimes," he said.

"For years, I told my daughter that I was in the helicopter," Jeff said about the fire that Dave Harrison directed him out of on May 3, 1992. A color photograph taken that day shows Dave's chopper and a large fireball to the left of the helicopter. It hangs on the mantel in Jeff's home. He was under that fireball when the radios fell silent.

The fire burned 4,832 acres, but the good thing that came out of it, Jeff reminded me, is that no lives or man-made structures were lost—an incredible fact considering the intensity of the fire.

Fires that scorch more than 100 acres require the section warden to complete a major fire report that gets critiqued by the division warden and all his supervisors. Jeff was still completing his report on the May 1992 fire when the woods ignited again.

It was June 13, 1992, and Lacey was burning again. As the fire headed toward Double Trouble State Park, Jeff was concerned about the nearby homes. The fire started to move into the cranberry bogs and lowlands, which were dry because the streams had been blocked in preparation for the fall harvest.

Jeff immediately moved to open the flood gates and flood the bogs. The superintendent for Double Trouble said he would see if he could get approval to open the gates. "I got all the approval I need right here," Jeff replied, motioning to the fire starting to lick at the edges of the park.

The flooded bogs, along with the area that had been scorched the month before, starved the fire of fuel and helped choke it out. Still, 5,400 acres were lost.

"The Pine Barrens burn hotter and faster than any place else in the U.S., and that's a documented fact," Jeff told me. "Out West, it can take 3 days for 10,000 acres to burn. Here, they can burn in 3 hours."

Jeff should know. He has put out fires in every state west of the Mississippi and has been away from home anywhere from 3 weeks to 6 months.

"You can't equate West Coast stuff with East Coast stuff," he said. "It's two different worlds." He recalled that out West, he was required to wear Nomex fire retardant pants, shirt, boots, hardhat, and a shroud for the back of the neck. In the Pine Barrens, his usual attire for fighting fires was blue jeans, a T-shirt, and sneakers. After Jeff arrived back in Jersey, the supervisor told the men that they should wear boots and asked Jeff where his were. "Home," he replied without missing a beat. "Let me tell you something, if my truck catches fire, I can run faster in sneakers than I can in boots."

It was this grittiness that kept Jeff alive and fueled his determination to bring his crew out alive every time. His resilience comes from surviving close calls and the responsibility he bore as a section warden.

State geologists believe that in the late 1800s, 70,000 to 100,000 acres burned annually in the Pine Barrens. The New Jersey Forest Fire Service was established on April 18, 1906, and falls under the jurisdiction of the Department of Environmental Protection. Today, approximately 1,600 wildfires erupt in New Jersey each year.[1]

Division B encompasses all of Mercer, Monmouth, Ocean, and Burlington counties, as well as the southern half of Middlesex County. It is the hottest division in the state. Section 5—the one Jeff was in charge of in 1992—covers a little more than 100,000 acres and includes parts of Woodland, Barnegat, Ocean, Lacey, and Manchester townships.

"I was always taught that you can survive a fire being in your truck," Jeff said. "One time, I almost burnt up when I was alone … when I went in to attack the fire. I'm working the hose and driving, and this pine tree came in through the window—just a little thing— and it went underneath my arm and jacked me up to the roof of the truck. Then the truck stalled, but I am so grateful; otherwise, it would have ripped my arm off.

"I called Jeffrey and told him I needed help. Then it all got smoky and started getting hot. I lay down—how I got my arm out from being stuck, I have no idea. All of a sudden, the fire turned very yellow and orangey, so I reached up and pushed the clutch with my hand. I turned the key, started the truck, and grabbed the steering wheel real quick. I switched hands, turned to the left, and hit the gas pedal as hard as I could and drove right out through the middle of the burn. Once out, I sat up and the truck stalled out again. Whew! I was safe—the fire was back behind me.

"I had driven through it. I lost the tree somewhere along the line, the windshield, the paint job, and a few other things. That was one of the real close ones—that was back around 1988, and it was not a big fire, only 5 or 10 acres, but you don't need to have a giant fire [for it] to kill you."

Jeff explained that when you start with a smaller fire, you have to stop the spread. He told me that you don't really attack it from the head; you attack it from one of the flanks by driving around it counter-clockwise. You start out from the flank, move up toward the head, and then come all the way back around.

"I was taught, when I first started, that the driver's side should never be more than 3 feet from the fire's edge," Jeff said. "If you were any farther away than that, then you were chicken, and you shouldn't be doing that type of work. The trucks are designed so that you can pull the hose up from the back and stick your arm out the window. That way, you can squirt the water as you drive around the fire.

"The first thing is to stop the forward spread of the fire. You're just trying to knock it down to a point where you can contain it or you can manage working with it until the rest of your personnel can get in and put control lines around it—whether that be by hand or by actually letting it burn to the road or by using a tractor and plow."

The Forest Fire Service uses John Deere 350s to plow fire breaks right down to the mineral soil so that nothing can burn underground or across the line. "It helps it to burn out quicker if you have all those plow lines in," Jeff said.

"When you get into fire suppression, if you are going to use back-fires for a fire break, you have to know how to get far enough ahead of it so that when it starts throwing spot fires, you are prepared. You have to know enough about fire behavior to know how far to get ahead of it. With the May 1992 fire, all four lanes of the Garden State Parkway didn't amount to a bicycle path; it jumped all four lanes.

"As a fire burns, it leans over in a curl much the way an ocean wave does. As it builds momentum, rising into the tree canopy, it sucks up more oxygen. It picks up an unbelievable updraft. As it devours the underbrush, pine trees, and other fuel, the burning embers are drawn upward and carried along by the 'wave,' or curl of fire. When they become too heavy, they drop to the ground, igniting smaller, spot fires."

Shooting the curl means driving right through the heart of the fire, directly underneath that leaning fireball that threatens to burn anything in its path.

"Fire is a living, breathing animal," Jeff said. "You have to respect what it can and will do." He says he relives the May 1992 fire every day of his life. But he reminds me that he had the greatest career in the world, in his opinion.

"A lot of people ask, why do you want to do this? I say, you are either gonna love it or hate it—and if you hate it, you don't belong there."

Endnote

1. Section Forest Firewardens of Division B, *Images of America: New Jersey Forest Fire Service* (Charleston, SC: Arcadia Publishing, 2006), 7–9.

Snared

Physically, Newt Sterling must strike many people as the quintessential New Jersey Piney. Fifty-eight years old and standing 5-foot-2, with a salt-and-pepper beard and moustache, he was clad in jeans and a T-shirt touting his company, Snare One, the day we met. Emblazoned in the center of the shirt was the company logo—a caricature of himself and the words *Piney Power*.

Newt is a man who has learned not to take himself (or life) too seriously, a lesson at which most of us need to keep working. His solid frame and tanned skin bespeak the amount of time he spends outdoors.

My first test came when I arrived on Newt's property. His directions were excellent; most Pineys can probably get you to their doorsteps from 50 miles in any direction—that is if they want to. R. Marilyn Schmidt is often asked for directions by those stopping at her store, Buzby's, in Chatsworth. She recalls one time, after she had just given precise directions to an out-of-towner, a local who was in the store at the time declared that Marilyn was no Piney. "What do you mean?" she asked, to which the local dryly replied, "A true Piney would have sent him the opposite way."

Newt's directions were perfect, however, right down to the turn-off for his dirt driveway. He'd warned me his place was a mess, and I'd said it didn't matter to me. I pulled up alongside a cherry tree to which a sign that read "Beware of Bear Traps" had been nailed, parked the car, and headed toward the house. I tried knocking, then ringing the bell. No answer. I decided to try calling him on my cell phone.

"Over here," came his voice through the receiver. I scanned the numerous trailers and buildings on the lot and finally spotted a hand waving from a trailer toward the back. I picked my way carefully between the snares and traps that covered the ground. Newt's dog Brick, a Lakeland terrier, jumped and ran alongside me, apparently hoping for a scratch on the head.

Inside the trailer, I could see that Newt had been busy cutting snares. He moved some papers off a chair and invited me to sit, then took a seat across from me. My chair was elevated, almost like a bar stool, and I found myself in the awkward position of looking down at him while we spoke.

Somewhat cautiously, Newt began to tell me about his trade, snare trapping. He explained that the secret of his success was learning and understanding an animal's behavior. He chose his words carefully, not completely sure of my purpose or my position on animal trapping and snaring. At times, he quizzed me on my knowledge of the industry. About an hour into our discussion, it hit me that he had been sizing me up, determining how much he could trust me, just as he did animals in the wild. I began to understand why he was so successful in his work.

Newt is recognized as one of the North America's leading snare and trap experts; he is also "widely regarded as one of the most experienced baymen in South Jersey."[1] As he shared his expertise, it occurred to me that if I were to be stranded in the woods or on the water, I couldn't do better than to have Newt as a traveling companion.

Newt's quiet, steadfast demeanor as he took my measure obviously serves him well in the outdoors. He's a man who knows how to take risks and survive. Having practically grown up on the bay, he is as comfortable on the water as most of us are in our living rooms.

Almost as an afterthought, Newt shared a story about a close brush with death. It began on a 38-degree morning in January 2004, when he and two companions—Bob Jameson, age 52, and John Scagline, age 54, along with Bob's Lab-golden retriever mix, Max—set course for the Edwin B. Forsythe Wildlife Refuge to check the traps they had set for predators such as otters, foxes, and raccoons. Newt had been hired by the U.S. Fish and Wildlife Service to trap these predators with a cable restraining snare to prevent them from eating the eggs of the endangered piping plover. Their vessel was a garvey, built by Newt.

Without warning, a high wave and a freak wind combined to catch and flip the boat, instantly plunging the three men and the dog into the 45-degree water. Not only were the men at immediate risk for hypothermia, but this part of the bay was isolated from most boat traffic.

Bob asked Newt: "What are the chances we'll be seen?"

With the sense of acceptance that Pineys seem to instinctively feel, Newt said, "I'm sorry, I killed you guys today."[2]

I have heard this calmness in men talking about the death of a child at an age too early for comprehension or describing a house fire that destroyed everything they owned. It is this solid determination, this oneness with the cycles of nature, that has enabled generations of New Jersey Pineys and baymen to live off the land and remain in harmony with it. And it was this understanding that allowed Newt and his companions to remain calm in the January bay waters. They made small talk to boost spirits, they advised one another against taking dangerous risks, and—most important—they each put the interests of the others ahead of their own.

The motor dragged one end of the garvey into the bay's frigid depths, and it now rested on the bottom. This left about 5 feet of the hull protruding awkwardly into the air at an angle, which the men tried to climb onto. John, a severe diabetic, was in particular peril. He was unable to get onto the hull because of the strong, rocking waves. As hypothermia took over and his speech began to slur, Bob knew they had to get him out of the water somehow.

They remembered the canoe that had been lashed to the top of the garvey and began to dive to free it. Even though they knew this extra exertion would decrease their chances of survival, the men plunged in anyway. After several attempts, Newt and Bob managed to free the small canoe from the bottom, but efforts to place John in it failed. Each time they tried to lift John, whose waterlogged clothing nearly doubled his weight, into the canoe, it would roll and spill him back into the water. On the third try, they got John halfway into the canoe, but as it rolled over again, it pitched John into the water once more. As Newt and Bob dove for John, the canoe drifted away toward the shore. The trio began to make their final petitions to God. Newt recalled being filled with peace as he reflected on a lifetime of doing what he loved every day.

They had been in the water for 3 hours when the captain of a distant boat on a waterfowl hunt caught sight of the wayward canoe. He couldn't quite make it out, but he knew the tan shape was not part of the natural landscape and immediately followed an unwritten bayman's law that anything unnatural is investigated. Reaching the canoe, he began a search for its origin and soon turned up the three men, only a hundred yards away but tucked out of sight. Had it not been for the canoe and the Herculean efforts of Newt and Bob to free it in an attempt to help John, they would not have been discovered.

Newt's and Bob's core temperatures had fallen to 92 degrees, but amazingly, they were both discharged from the hospital within hours of admission. John hadn't fared so well: His body temperature had plummeted to 80 degrees, and his liver had started to shut down. Miraculously, he was talking later that afternoon, walking that evening, and able to leave the hospital the following day. The doctor said that given John's diabetes and the hypothermic conditions he endured, he should not have survived. His wife told the doctor, "He's a hunter and a trapper. These men are a breed apart."

Speaking of breeds, I was happy to learn that 8-year-old Max survived as well.

When I asked Newt to what he credited his survival, he said, "Not panicking." As I got to know him that day, exploring his environs and watching videotapes of his trapping expeditions, I realized that the ability to stay calm under pressure was hardwired into his nature.

Newt's father was a hunter and trapper too. During the Great Depression, it was a dependable way to make money relative to other jobs, though Newt said his dad viewed it as something of a hobby. When World War II broke out and most of the local men headed off to war, their trapping days came to an abrupt end.

With all the traps lying around, it wasn't long before young Newt and his cousins got into a friendly trapping competition. The years passed, and Newt married and started a family. He got into construction, building houses, cabinets, and boats—the sort of work that could put meals on the table and sustain a growing family. Once his children were out on their own, Newt returned to full-time trapping.

"I don't need much money for me to be happy. As long as I can pay the bills," he said, "I'd rather travel around the country than be stuck here with a heavy job and a lot of debts."

It hasn't always been easy, but through perseverance, Newt has managed to support himself. In addition to the money he makes trapping, he runs a successful business called Snare One. Through an ecommerce website, Newt sells the snares and traps he builds, as well as instructional videos, scents, lures, and other supplies. "Trappers prefer to make their own stuff," he told me as he showed me drawers of locks, cables, springs, and assorted hardware.

It seems as if most of the Pineys I've talked with have hunted or trapped at some point in their lives, but Newt was the first person I'd talked to who seemed to eat, breathe, and sleep trapping. I asked him what it was that set him apart from other trappers. As I listened to him speak passionately about his trade, I couldn't picture him doing anything else; clearly, there's nothing else he'd rather be doing.

Newt believes that trappers are born, not made. He shared a story with me about hunting with his dad. As the two headed out to check their traps, Newt would predict, "This one will have a red fox in it, that one will have a gray fox." He was correct with alarming regularity, and his father couldn't figure out how he did it.

"He thought I was a genius," Newt said, "but it was because of the size of the snare I set, the location, and the habitat—red fox like it more open, gray fox more tight and thick with briars and all. It was just a matter of reading the location and knowing where these animals were going to be—that's all it was."

Newt's education came from two areas: experience in the wild and formalized schooling. He went to a professional trappers' college in LaGrange, Indiana, and qualified to be an instructor. The college is sanctioned by Purdue University, where Newt taught for a while.

He still continues to teach on an informal basis, and I was impressed with his homemade videos, especially the close-up shots of a properly set snare, along with detailed instructions—even advice on which store aisles to look in for specific supplies. These videos are not without their lighter moments. In one, Newt almost gets bitten by a raccoon; in another, as the credits roll, there's an outtake of someone greeting him while he's wrapping things up. "You messed up my filming!" he jokes good-naturedly.

According to Newt, the hardest part of the job isn't figuring out how to trap a particular animal; it's the environmental conditions. "It's the mud, the snow, the muck—that's where you can get into trouble," he explained. "If you're inland, and you get all set up and then it rains for a week and the rivers rise, you're done. I went to a location in Mississippi a few years back. I got everything set up, and another trapper saw me and said, 'You better get your traps up within the next 3 days.' I asked him why, and he told me that there had been torrential rains in Minnesota, and when that happens, it takes 3 days for the river to rise where we were. I heeded his advice, but not before telling him that he had water that's 'unnatural' in his state. What I meant was that it only flowed one way. At least on the coast, it flows both ways," Newt laughed.

If there's anything I learned about Newt from speaking with him and then watching him on his videos, it's that he has an amazing sense of humor. I imagine it serves him well as he trudges through that mud, snow, and muck en route to his trapping grounds.

Being at the mercy of the weather is not the only hardship. "It's the long drives, being willing to be uncomfortable most of the time, long hours, lack of sleep, and not much money." Trapping also involves reinventing the wheel, so to speak. "Trappers are always looking to build the better mousetrap," Newt said. "There's not a lot of money in trapping unless you get a big paying job, like a ranch. You have to have the ability to adapt and redesign. It's really tough to trap in one area and then pick up and go to another. Even the pros will tell you that in the first year, you don't look to make a profit—if you break even, you're lucky. The following year, you'll pick up more land to trap, and you'll know how to trap that area a little better. Each year should get a little better, and you'll continue making profits as you go."

Newt traps for two reasons: demand for fur and animal damage control. As he explained the particulars of each, I got an education on what trapping is really all about. As I traveled around the Pine

Barrens talking to Newt and the other individuals who make their living off the land, I learned that they have an enormous respect for the environment. They know that if they don't take care of the land, the consequences will impact both their stock in trade and their ability to pass it on to their children and grandchildren. Individuals like Newt Sterling and Steve Lee truly have become stewards of the land.

Newt took the time to show me many of his snares and traps, explaining what each was used for and how it worked and offering a demonstration. Next, I learned that Americans have never been the main market for fur coats and hats, and we make up less than 20 percent of buyers worldwide. "Fur has always been a foreign market," Newt said. "Mainly Europe, but now Asia is coming into the ball game as those economies are lifting up."

"Trapping is actually America's oldest profession," Newt informed me. "This country was founded on it." He gave me more food for thought. Let's say you are a vegetarian and don't eat meat or don't wear fur—what value does trapping offer you? Do you live in a house made with wood beams? Do you own wood furniture? Do you ever use a pencil?

If the answer is yes, you are dependent on the trapping industry. Beaver build dams that cause rivers to rise, and timber companies, especially down South, hire trappers to keep the beaver populations in check. "If the water level rises a foot, it doesn't flood an acre or two; it floods thousands," Newt said. "Then the water on the tree trunks will kill the trees themselves if there is enough [water] there for a while. The timber industry down South is a huge industry, so they've got to protect the trees. Trees down there are like a crop of corn to us in the North."

Among the most interesting things I learned from Newt was the meaning of *carrying capacity*. Some may call it the *circle of life* or *balance of nature*. The term was first used in 1845 in the shipping industry and refers to the number of individuals that can be supported positively in a particular environment. In the case of an animal population that grows too large for a specific area, food sources will run out, and some animals will starve to death. Some animals will even kill their own species to survive when food becomes scarce, which helps explain why so many species are territorial; nature has endowed them with a powerful survival instinct.

Most hunters will tell you that thinning out excess populations—whether to offset imbalances caused by human development, the loss of habitat, or for other reasons—is a humane practice. "Mother Nature can be very cruel," Newt said.

We talked about the overpopulation of red fox on Island Beach State Park that occurred a few years ago after summer tourists, stuck in traffic, began feeding the foxes along the highway. "They all died because of carrying capacity—you can't put 40 ounces of water in a quart jar; that's all it is," Newt said somberly. "To protect that fox herd, you have to harvest it, and you would have had a healthy fox herd the whole time. When Mother Nature came in to rebalance things, she gave rabies and distemper and parvo, and the fox died a long, suffering death."

It's funny, but Newt got me thinking that the same people who believe in compassionate euthanasia and will put a beloved family pet to sleep rather than see it suffer are often the most outspoken against hunting and trapping.

One thing we should all ask in our own communities is what form of animal control, including hunting and trapping, is the most appropriate. Speaking of the coyotes and black bear that are currently making a comeback in the region, Newt said, "They were here first; we [moved in] on their home. It's not vice versa—we screwed up their natural habitat, so now we have to control their habitat so we can live around them."

Newt then gave me the following scenario to think about. He played a 20-second sound clip for me and asked me to identify it. I thought it sounded like a newborn's cries. It was actually a rabbit crying out in the brush. "If a coyote hears a baby cry and thinks he's hearing a food source [and attacks], he's not doing anything wrong—he's just trying to eat," he explained. "He's not attacking a human; he's after food. And an animal with cubs to feed is very dangerous."

What if you have a small child in an area where killing coyotes has been outlawed and their population is on the rise? Suddenly, the line between animal cruelty and the need to protect our own, to ensure the survival of our species, becomes blurred. Whose backyard is it anyway? It's clear there are some hard questions we have to ask before weighing in on animal control.

Animals are highly adaptive creatures and will adjust to the environment, even a human one, to survive. Generally, if an animal has learned to fear guns and hunters, it will do its best to avoid people. However, if it has come to regard campers as an easy food source, it will become emboldened. According to Newt, "The sound of a chainsaw up in Maine when it's real cold and nasty out will draw deer because they know they can eat the tops off the trees that were felled."

Newt's biggest challenge is not so much dealing with a specific species of animal as dealing with how experienced an individual animal is. This is what makes animal control more difficult than fur trapping. "In fur trapping, we want to come in and take off the cream of the crop and move on. When you get into damage control, the fur trapper has already come in and taken off the cream, and now you are dealing with the old, seasoned adults who have been around for years. The only reason they're around is because they are a lot smarter than the pups.

"When teaching fur trapping, I get asked a lot, 'How do you catch this coyote that's doing this and doing that?' and I say, 'You pick up your traps and go to the next farm, and you'll catch 10 dumb ones because where I come from, 10 dumb ones are worth 10 times more than one smart one.'"

Some animals will become trap shy—a learned behavior, Newt says. "They smell the lure and find an animal dead at that spot, and then they come back later and find another one dead in that spot, and a day or two later, another one dead. I don't know what they are thinking, but if I saw all my relatives lying dead in the same spot ...

"I was up in Canada at a convention several years ago. A biologist told us that the province warned hikers about wolves in the area. It suggested hikers carry pepper spray and wear bells on their shoes. The biologist told us that he had done a study on wolf scat in the area and could tell the difference between an animal kill and a human kill by examining the wolf scat. I said, 'How is that?' and he replied that the scat from a human kill smelled like pepper and had little bells in it."

As I packed up to leave, Newt left me with these final thoughts: "God gave animals to us to use, not abuse. If you travel in trapper circles, you'll find that trappers know more about animals and are more animal-loving than anybody you'll ever meet. To catch these animals effectively, we got to know everything about them."

Endnotes

1. Bob Noonan, "Defying Death," *The Trapper and Predator Caller*, January 2005, 22–26.
2. Ibid.

RADONS

Although it happened more than 20 years ago, Cyndy Book clearly remembers the evening of Thursday, June 4, 1987. She had just come home, flopped down on the couch, and turned on the evening news, as was her habit. There was one of those quick news stories—the two- or three-liners jammed in just before the commercial break. The newscaster was saying that 15,000 drums of radon-contaminated soil were to be deposited at the Colliers Mills Wildlife Management Area the following day. The report showed pictures of large dump trucks, and then the commercials came on.

Cyndy stared at the TV in disbelief—had she heard right? She frantically began making phone calls, but no one seemed to know anything about it. So she climbed into her truck and drove out to the entrance of the refuge, just 6 miles from her home in New Egypt.

Cyndy practically grew up in these woods. Fair-skinned, of average height, her long strawberry-blonde hair usually parked under a baseball cap, she looks the part of an outdoorswoman. Her lean frame disguises the fact that she works as a bricklayer. Though she may strike strangers as somewhat quiet and shy, Cyndy can take care of herself.

She has probably walked every trail in Colliers Mills and has made a point of learning about wildlife because she feels the only way to protect it is to become knowledgeable about it. To this end, she has enrolled in Department of Environmental Protection (DEP) courses on surveying for threatened and endangered species, and she also studies field and tracking guides. She would like to see teachers at schools located near the Pine Barrens take students on field trips so that children can learn about "pine snakes, cranberry bogs, and the history of the Pine Barrens."

Cyndy's love for these woods and the wildlife within them is unmistakable. The Pines may be the last place many of us would think of going on a 90-degree day, but those who have hiked these woods in the summer know that the temperature drops significantly inside the tree line—the result of a process known as *evapotranspiration*. That said, even hikers don't generally make a point of heading to the woods when the temperature spikes. Cyndy does.

Apart from the quiet that comes from the emptiness of a place such as Colliers Mills on a hot day, there are other benefits that those of us relaxing inside air-conditioned rooms miss out on. As Cyndy tells it, "You can go out to Colliers Mills on a day when it's in the 90s, and there are all these flies and the bugs. It's horrible in certain places on a hot day, but when you walk into a cedar swamp and the temperature drops, you feel like you are walking into a refrigerated room. With the root system in a cedar swamp, you're walking above the water, but if you're not careful, you can fall through. The spaces between the roots fill in with spongy green sphagnum moss and tiny little flowers—it's very much like walking through a fairy land."

Having walked cedar swamps with Cyndy (and, yes, I did manage to sink into one and personally experience the "quicksand effect" she had warned me about), I can easily understand why she was so concerned about the radon threat to Colliers Mills. As she approached the entrance to the refuge on the night of the news broadcast, others who had heard the story were also gathering and questioning each other: "What did you hear?" "Do you know anything more about this?" No one did, but it was clear early on, Cyndy said, that everyone present would do what was necessary to prevent the dumping.

Because those who had gathered didn't know when the trucks would arrive, a number of them decided to park there overnight and sleep in their vehicles so that they would be ready. In the morning, more people began to arrive.

The trucks carrying crushed gravel arrived on Saturday. A line of vehicles prevented their entry, and the New Jersey State Police were called in. As Cyndy tells it, no one wanted to get arrested, but the protestors were determined to stop the trucks, so when the police told them to move their vehicles, they did—but not very far.

According to Cyndy, the first truck to get through was a big rig with a brand-new paint job. When it emerged from the woods, the driver got out and told the other truckers, "It was horrible, guys, don't go back there—my brand-new rig is ruined—the branches scratched the paint." As he stood there shaking his head and looking at his truck, some of the other drivers turned and left the scene.

Cyndy and two men sat down cross-legged in the middle of the entrance road. The police physically picked them up and relocated them. The two men were arrested and handcuffed, but the officers did not arrest Cyndy. I asked whether she knew why. "Maybe because I looked terrified?" she suggested. "Because I was."

A third man was then arrested for letting the air out of the front tire of a police bus that had been brought to the scene in case numerous arrests became necessary. Another protester drove down the road and got her car "stuck" in the deep, soft sugar sand. The police were not amused and insisted she move her vehicle. She and her husband complied, pushing the vehicle out by hand.

By now the crowd of protestors had swelled into the hundreds. A core group of people, with Cyndy among the unofficial leaders, began to plan their next moves. Some volunteered to contact the media, others to call on local politicians. Soon, news reporters arrived; stories of the protest and the dumping plan became headline fodder for weeks afterward.

***

Where had the radon-contaminated soil come from? And who decided to dump it in the Pine Barrens? To answer these questions, we must go back to 1898, when radium was first discovered by Marie Curie in Paris. After years of research and lab work with her husband, Pierre, Marie presented her findings in her doctoral thesis on June 25, 1903. The committee described her report as "the greatest scientific contribution ever made in a doctoral thesis."[1]

A celebration was thrown in the Curies' honor that evening. Pierre had a little surprise for the group; he pulled a tube of radium salt in solution from his waistcoat, and the tube began to glow. One of the party noticed that Pierre's hands shook as he held the tube. It would be learned later that as they continued working in the lab, the couple's health began to fail, which at the time everyone attributed to their long hours rather than to radiation poisoning. In 1903, the Curies were awarded half of the Nobel Prize in physics for their work.[2]

It was Marie who coined the term *radioactivity*. Despite the deaths of colleagues from leukemia, she contended the chemicals they were working with were safe. Radium does not exist freely in nature; the Curies extracted it from the mineral pitchblende. It is a particularly unstable chemical element that starts out as uranium, decays into radon, and finally ends up as lead, emitting particles and energy along the way. Marie worked to purify it as a radiation treatment for tumors.

Radium's bluish glow-in-the-dark properties caught the public's attention, and soon the U.S. began extracting it for use in novelties. Radium-painted luminous dials on wristwatches became a huge fad in the mid-1910s. Radium Luminous Materials Corp. became the first large corporation to produce such watches when it opened in 1917 in Orange, New Jersey. Using a technique called *lip-pointing*, women workers used their lips and tongues to shape the paintbrush tip—undoubtedly ingesting large amounts of the chemical.[3] In addition, many painted their nails, eyelids, and teeth with it to take advantage of the glowing effects.[4]

By the 1920s, women working in the plant were becoming sick and dying in increasing numbers. Dentists trying to remove diseased teeth from the women found chunks of jawbone coming loose as well. The term *radium jaw* was coined in 1923 when five women who worked in the Orange factory died from this condition.[5]

The bodies of many women working in the Orange plant, and in ones like it in Illinois and Connecticut, became radioactive. When radium is taken into the body, it forms chemical bonds in the same pattern as calcium does. It is then absorbed into the bones and emits radiation, causing bone tumors, anemia, or leukemia. Marie Curie is believed to have died from either anemia or leukemia.[6]

In 1925, the Orange County medical examiner linked the diseases contracted by the women to the paint they were dipping their brushes in, and by 1926, Radium Luminous Materials Corp. was shut down. The corporation had also operated as an extraction plant. Parents gathered the finely textured waste ore, referred to as the *tailings*, as play sand for children.[7] This "sand" was also used as landfill for the low-lying areas of the surrounding New Jersey towns of Glen Ridge, Montclair, and West Orange. Housing developments were built on top of the 210-acre landfill during the 1920s and 1930s.[8]

Fifty years later, the Superfund law was enacted as a response to the Comprehensive Environmental Response, Compensation, and

Liability Act of 1980. The law allows the Environmental Protection Agency (EPA) to identify and clean up abandoned hazardous waste sites and bill responsible parties for the expense.[9] The law was enacted following the Love Canal disaster in New York, where, in the 1950s, homes were built atop a landfill containing hazardous waste. Twenty years later, the contents of the rotted drums began percolating up through the soil following a heavy rainfall.[10]

In 1981, a federal aerial survey located excess gamma radiation—a by-product of radium decay—in Glen Ridge, Montclair, and West Orange, all within a 12-mile range of the old Radium Luminous Materials Corp. site.[11] The presence of radioactive soil was confirmed by the EPA in 1983, and the area was added to the Superfund list 4 years later.

Radon gas is not considered dangerous in the open; however, when it becomes concentrated inside a home, it can cause lung cancer in those who inhale it. The EPA initially installed lead shields and ventilation systems in the area's most seriously contaminated homes, some with radon levels 100 times the level deemed safe by the agency.

Approximately 5,000 cubic yards of soil was excavated from around and under these homes and placed in 15,000 50-gallon drums in 1983. The original plan was to ship the soil to a licensed low-level waste disposal facility in Beatty, Nevada. Nevada reneged on the agreement, according to DEP Commissioner Richard T. Dewling, because "the radium concentrations were too low and the soil was too clean to justify the space it would take up in a facility designed for waste that needs to be contained."[12]

So instead, 10,000 of the drums were stored on a railroad siding in Kearny and the other 5,000 around homes in Montclair.[13] The idea of shipping the waste to the Pinelands first surfaced in 1985. In a memorandum titled "Temporary Storage of Radium-Contaminated Waste at McGuire Air Force Base," New Jersey Pinelands

Commission executive director Terrence D. Moore wrote to Franklin E. Parker, chairperson of the Commission:

> Based upon the provisions of the comprehensive management plan, I must conclude that the proposed temporary storage of radium-contaminated soils within the boundaries of the New Jersey Pinelands cannot be accomplished. I would also suggest that such an undertaking would run counter to both the spirit and provisions of the Pinelands Protection Act and the National Park and Recreation Act of 1978.[14]

In June 1986, the DEP sought to develop a quarry site in Vernon Township as a soil-blending facility and ship the contaminated soil there, but enormous local opposition arose.

Essex County Superior Court Judge Murray G. Simon set a deadline of June 15, 1987, for the DEP to remove the drums from Montclair and relocate them. The removal was ordered because the drums could impede access to the homes by emergency vehicles or personnel.

The DEP first offered the town of Kearny $6.8 million from the Superfund to store the drums temporarily, but the town council voted against the idea. The DEP then planned to use a cleared wildlife grazing site in the Colliers Mills Wildlife Management Area as a "temporary solution" until a permanent home could be found for the barrels of soil. The site was adjacent to the U.S. Air Force BOMARC (named for its developers, Boeing and the Michigan Aeronautical Research Center) missile site, where a BOMARC nuclear missile warhead was melted by an underground missile fire on June 7, 1960, contaminating the area with plutonium.[15,16]

DEP Assistant Commissioner for hazardous waste management John W. Gaston Jr., announced that Waste Conversion, Inc., of Hatfield, Pennsylvania—the state's contractor—had agreed to work

7 days a week so that all 15,000 barrels could be relocated within 2 weeks. "The department looked for a site that was extremely rural, a tract of state-owned land that was not in proximity to a residential area," Gaston said. "This temporary storage meets those guidelines."

***

Daniel J. ("Dan") Black was only 31 years old in 1987. It was his first year as mayor of Jackson Township, where the majority of Colliers Mills is located. He had been a committeeman for 2 years and then served as deputy mayor in 1986. He thought the biggest part of his new role would be to marry people.

Dan was working on the construction of his new home when he heard the news. He and his older brother were unloading doors for the house when someone came by to tell him to call Senator Leonard T. Connors right away.

Dan went into the house in the front of the lot, where he and his wife, Vickie, were living. He called the senator's office and was told to come down immediately for a press conference. Dan stopped what he was doing and headed down to the office, leaving his brother to finish unloading the truck.

When he arrived, Senator Connors and Freeholder George Buckwald quickly filled him in on the DEP's plans to dispose of the radium-contaminated soil in Colliers Mills.[17] "We all agreed from the get-go that this was unacceptable," Dan said. The date was June 4, 1987.

At the press conference, Senator Connors said he "was outraged at a system that would rope off an area for tree frogs and pine snakes, but store hazardous waste in the heart of it all. It seems that only the DEP is allowed to screw up the environment."[18]

The Jackson Township Committee called an emergency public meeting at the municipal building at 8 PM. All five members of the committee—Peter Carlson, Bruce Cottrell, Roslyn Olsen, Deputy Mayor Mel Cottrell, and Dan—were present. Dan opened the meeting by stating that he had become aware of the problem at 2:15 that afternoon, when Senator Connors contacted him. He read a letter into the minutes from Senator Connors to DEP Commissioner Dewling, dated October 16, 1986. The letter was accompanied by four newspaper clippings discussing state plans to dump the waste and read as follows:

> Attached are four news clippings. It appears that a candidate in the 13th Congressional District race is charging that the state has plans to dispose of radon-contaminated soil at McGuire Air Force Base in Plumsted Township off Route 539.
>
> We are compelled to take this opportunity to state clearly our opposition to any pending decisions which would threaten health and welfare of the citizens of our district or the environment.
>
> At your earliest convenience, we request from you a full disclosure of all circumstances associated with or related to the allegations in these clippings. Finally, we would respectfully ask your office to maintain direct and immediate contact with us on this issue in the future.
>
> Thank you in advance for your prompt attention to this matter, as it has become an issue of serious concern.

Dewling's response, dated November 14, 1986, read as follows:

> This is in response to your letter of October 16, 1986, in which you expressed concern regarding recent newspaper articles indicating that the Department of Environmental Protection is considering disposal of soil containing trace amounts of radium at a site near Plumstead [sic]

Township. The specific site mentioned is an inactive BOMARC missile site associated with McGuire Air Force Base but actually located on the Fort Dix Military Reservation. This site is contaminated with radioactive plutonium-239 as a result of a fire which occurred in 1968 and which involved a nuclear warhead mounted on a BOMARC missile.

I wish to assure you that we do not consider such a proposal as technically feasible or environmentally sound. In fact, we rejected it out of hand when it was suggested to us over a year ago. It is our position that the BOMARC site is contaminated and must be restored to an environmentally sound condition without any additional complications. We, therefore, have no plans to request the use of this site from the Department of Defense for any purpose whatsoever. We are continuing in our efforts to have the Air Force restore this site to a safe and environmentally sound condition.

Thank you for your interest in this issue.

Dan read the letters into the minutes to document Dewling's contradiction and so that the committee would have a basis for taking further action. Then Dan said, "We will use any legal means we can to stop this. The township committee, myself, and the residents of Jackson Township find this unacceptable and totally outrageous. Historically, Central Jersey has been dumped on by North Jersey. I feel it just has to be stopped."

Committeeperson Olsen likened this "despicable act" to a "sneak Pearl Harbor Attack" and stated that the committee would not accept it.[19] Deputy Mayor Cottrell called for the resignation of Commissioner Dewling. His motion was seconded by Committeeperson Carlson and accepted unanimously by the committee. It was further decided that a rally would take place at 11:00 the next morning at town hall, after which, residents and committee members would go to the site and protest. The meeting was adjourned only 40 minutes after it began.

On Friday, June 5, Jackson residents gathered at Town Hall. Vickie Black recalls the crowd being angry initially; those who had not attended the previous night's meeting assumed that the township was "in on it." When Dan took the microphone and announced that the DEP's action was unacceptable and they would fight it, a hush fell over the crowd.

Dan recalls that moment as a turning point. Once residents knew that the township was behind them, a lot of anger was dispelled, and the focus turned to unification. The crowd boarded buses and headed down to the entrance of Colliers Mills, where Cyndy and the others who had spent the night were gathered. To much applause, Dan told the crowd, "We are not going to be dumped on by North Jersey anymore!"

"I left Linden ten years ago to get away from the oil refineries," said 63-year-old retired truck driver William Machnowski. "The refineries didn't kill me, so now they want to kill me here."[20]

Trudi Brand, an employee of the Jackson Township tax assessor's office, was born in New York and moved to Jackson 12 years ago with her husband and two children. "People have no respect for us in Jackson," she said. "They think we're backwards, unsophisticated, but we have good schools and we all care for each other."[21]

The following day—Saturday, June 6—as trucks carrying crushed gravel for a temporary road roared to the site, state police were called. Dan knew the situation was a time bomb and could erupt into violence at any time. Keeping the crowd informed and calm became a primary focus.

The same day, Ocean County Superior Court Judge Eugene D. Serpentelli issued an injunction that temporarily barred the DEP from relocating the drums to Colliers Mills or delivering gravel to prepare the site. Twelve truckloads of gravel had been dumped before the injunction was issued; at that point, the remaining 50 trucks were turned away.

The temporary road had become necessary after actions of the freeholders the day before had closed two bridges that would have provided access to the site. County road crews removed the wooden planks from one bridge, located off Hawkin Road, on Friday. Meantime, county engineer Dick Lane said the other bridge, located off Route 571, should be restricted to vehicles weighing less than 4 tons to avoid potential collapse of the span. Freeholder Joseph Vicari insisted it was a coincidence that the bridges were restricted the day after word came of the DEP's plan.

Letters of support poured in from all over. The Jackson Environmental Commission said, in part, "we can sympathize with the residents of Montclair and Kearny and their eagerness to have the contaminated soil removed from their towns, but storage in the Pinelands, even temporary storage, is not the solution to the problem. A final resting place must be found. The practice of 'musical storage' must not be allowed to continue."

Formal motions filed in court by the township alleged that the soil posed "an immediate and irreparable threat to the ecosystem within the site and poses immediate and irreparable threat to the aquifer located beneath the site and to the health, safety and welfare of the residents of the Township of Jackson and surrounding areas."

The township further stated that "the Pinelands Preservation Law restricts any dumping or development with regard to toxic waste without proper permits and environmental impact statements ... and no environmental impact statement, hearings or any type of administrative procedure has been taken prior to the implementation of the administrative order transporting the contaminated soil to the site."

On June 8, 1987, approximately 500 people chanting "Hell no, we won't glow!" filed into the Jackson Municipal Building for another emergency meeting. Residents of Plumsted Township jammed their municipal building the same evening, voicing similar concerns about the dumping of waste in the wildlife area with an entrance that straddles the two townships' boundary lines at Hawkin Road.[22]

The following day, Dan got a call from Governor Tom Kean's chief of staff in response to Dan's request for a meeting. He was told that Kean would meet with him the next day at the Garden State Parkway administration building and that he could bring three people with him, but no press. Dan agreed and invited former Jackson Township Mayor Mel Cottrell, Senator Chris Mega's aide Loretta Charbonneau, and H. Jim Saxton's aide Sandy Condit to join him.

Dan was apprehensive about the meeting with the governor and went next door to speak to his father about it. "I remember pacing around a bit at my dad's welding shop and telling him about this meeting and how I was a little nervous. My dad was an old sage—an old Piney—and he told me, 'Son, just remember that the man puts his pants on one leg at a time, just like you do.' That calmed me down.

"The governor told me that this was pretty much the way it was going to be, and I told him that it couldn't stand, that we were just recovering from the Legler situation, as a result of accepting another town's waste. I told him how I had grown up near Legler and knew of someone whose daughter lost a kidney due to the problem." Legler was an area in Jackson where the dumping of toxic waste was linked to cancer and other illnesses. Residents won a $17.45 million settlement in July 1987.

"I told him that this was just going to escalate into something bad and that Dewling said that it just couldn't be shipped anywhere else—there was no other way to do it.

"I got a call from John Chando, president of TFC Nuclear Associates, who said, 'I guarantee that TFC Nuclear Associates will take these soils.' He said he tried to talk to Dewling, but no one would talk to him there. Commissioner Dewling says this can't be handled, but this company said they can do this. Kean thought that was very interesting, and he said he wasn't going to promise anything, but he would look into it."

U.S. representatives Saxton and Christopher Smith appealed to U.S. Interior Secretary Donald Hodel, who voiced his opposition to the plan on Wednesday, June 10, stating that it "would violate a unique ten year old partnership between the federal and state governments to protect what has been called the East Coast's last wilderness."[23]

The following Monday, June 15, Governor Kean announced the retention of former DEP Commissioner Richard J. Sullivan to "explore all options for a temporary storage site and eventual disposal of drums of dirt containing radon now being held in Montclair and Kearny."

Kean's statement went on to say, "The problem of storage and disposal of the dirt has reached such overwhelming proportions that it demands the full and complete attention of someone whose task will be to evaluate all proposals based on the best scientific, environmental and public safety data available. It is no longer a situation to which one can give divided attention and hope to develop an acceptable situation."[24]

The governor also said that Dewling and his staff were contending with other critical issues, such as solid waste disposal and the proposed clean oceans program.

On June 17, a New Jersey Appellate Division ruling upheld the injunction by Judge Serpentelli restraining the state from storing drums at Colliers Mills. In addition, the state was barred from doing any site preparation work.

That July, State Assemblyman John T. Hendrickson Jr. issued a statement in regard to criteria and assumptions made by the New Jersey Radium Radon Advisory Board. It read, "it should be pointed out that all ten of the DEP's own proposed and in-force regulations addressed here have been violated by the department in its attempt to store the radon soil in the Colliers Mills Wildlife Management Area."

He added, "Colliers Mills is dotted with lakes and streams, and the water table is never far below the surface. The aquifers underneath the refuge supply water for nearly all of Ocean County. The area around the refuge is so sensitive that local residents are prohibited from using fertilizer on plants or paving their driveways. ... The soil is so sandy and porous in the refuge that it is nearly impossible for a non-four-wheel-drive vehicle to travel to the proposed dump site. A person's foot at times will sink nearly to the ankle, as if on the beach at the ocean. This is an area that is inadequate in many places to support 200 pounds per square foot, much less 2,000."

Hendrickson went on to state, "the Colliers Mills refuge was purchased in the early 1940s using funds from the license fees of hunters and trappers. ... Using the public park system for non-preservation, non-recreational uses, particularly for the storage of a dangerous substance, severely damages the integrity and credibility of the Green Acres and other land purchase programs. What guarantees can Green Acres make to local officials and residents that this land will not be abused once it is placed in the hands of the DEP?"

The assemblyman's statement concluded, "if a private individual decided to rip down thousands of trees, plow a road three miles into a refuge, and discard 15,000 barrels of waste without any notice, permission, or environmental impact statement, he would be fined millions of dollars and face charges in court. With the powers granted to it as a public agency, the DEP has a responsibility not to abuse those powers. Its actions have been arbitrary and capricious. If this public agency were a private individual, it would probably be in jail. The public needs to be a part of the decision making process for a public agency."[25]

***

While all this was going on, activists and demonstrators had remained at the site to keep watch and continue to heighten public awareness. Cyndy said that the DeWolf family, who owned a farm in Plumsted, brought a large van-type vehicle to the site that they were able to use for storage.

"People were starting to ask what they could do, and somebody volunteered to go get the names and addresses of all our legislative officials ... not just local, but all over the state, because even people from out of state were coming down to check out our wildlife refuge to see what was going on," Cyndy said. "So we had a list of every single district in the state of New Jersey and who the legislators were, their phone numbers, and their mailing addresses.

"We started to form little committees to handle the different tasks—site watching, writing letters, contacting legislators and the media," she continued, "and the media asked if we had a name. So we decided to call ourselves RADONS—Residents Against Dumping of Noxious Soils. Soon there were articles in the papers almost every day, which was good, so people didn't forget what was going on.

"A lot of people wanted to help, but they were, like, 'Oh man, I gotta write a letter?'—we found out there's big-time apathy in sitting down to write a letter to anybody, so what we decided to do is write letters and put several blank lines on the bottom for personal comments. We sat there all day and all night; volunteers would come and hand out letters and say to people, 'Look, you can just sign this letter, but if you put a personal comment on it, then it's no longer a form letter because you are personalizing it,' so they would do that, but then a lot of times, it didn't seem like they would mail it, so we addressed and mailed them also." Cyndy explained that people donated paper, envelopes, and stamps.

RADONS became concerned that even though people came by the site every day and there was a core group of volunteers, if something big should happen—such as the injunction being lifted—how could they get a lot of people to the site quickly? Cyndy said they formed a phone chain, delegating people to call others in their area.

They had a false alarm one day, the result of a rumor that the trucks were coming. With no way to substantiate or disprove it, they put the phone chain into action to be on the safe side. "It was the coolest thing," Cyndy said. "Within 10 minutes there must have been 200 people at the site. Everybody agreed that it was really great to see that it worked; we weren't as worried if the trucks should suddenly show up or something. It gave us a little feeling of confidence that the system we theorized should work really worked."

RADONS had to overcome the NIMBY ("not in my back yard") objection after some people began to assert that the group was protesting simply because the dumping was proposed in their area. This is demonstrated in a legislative alert that was issued by Governor Kean's office:

> Despite its being non-hazardous, the material has been the subject of misunderstanding, misinformation, miscommunication, and misapprehension. The radon problem is now and must be addressed now. But it is part of a much larger issue. It is a precursor of what we in New Jersey—and the rest of the nation—will face in the coming years when the storage and disposal of truly hazardous materials is required. Our actions now, our cooperation now, our willingness to work together now to overcome the "not in my backyard" syndrome will be a key indicator of how successfully we can deal with these future problems.[26]

Cyndy stresses that theirs was not a NIMBY stance at all; Colliers Mills is recognized by both state and federal government as an environmentally sensitive piece of land, and legislation has been put in place to protect its wildlife and ecosystem. Dumping anything, she said, even harmless topsoil, would have been unacceptable to the protesters. "It was wrong. The wildlife refuge was not a dump—so even if it had been topsoil, people would still have fought it."

As the threat lingered throughout the summer, people were getting really tired. "It was getting harder to get people to stay overnight," Cyndy said. "It was summer, it was hot, there were a lot of mosquitoes, and people had jobs and lives to attend to." Besides the physical toll it was taking on Cyndy and the other RADONS, there was another concern.

"There was this one man who was making me very nervous … an older gentleman, maybe in his 50s," Cyndy recalls. "He was always there, but he wouldn't get involved with us; he was always standing there in the background, observing us, for what seemed like weeks. I thought he was a spy or something because he was very guarded in what he would say to us, but you could tell he was very observant, and he wore a radio on his side."

After several weeks, the man came up to Cyndy and identified himself as Ed Ryan from Ocean County Emergency Management. He said that his agency supported what RADONS was doing. "I have an offer to make, but you have really got to think about it," Ed said. He went on to explain that the Ocean County Mobile Command Unit had a big bus fitted with more than a million dollars' worth of equipment—protective gear, including hazardous waste suits, and radios to communicate with the Coast Guard, National Guard, Marine Corps, Army, Navy, Air Force, state and local police, and other military and civilian agencies. "We understand that you and your people could really use a place to hang out in and work, especially at night," Ed said. "We would be willing to let you use the mobile command unit and park it here, but somebody has to sign for it, which means you would be responsible if anything happens to it. I don't expect an answer right now, but I have been here watching for several weeks, and I feel that you are someone I'd be willing to let sign for it."

Only 24 at the time, Cyndy thought about how her future could be affected if anything were to happen to the bus. She talked about it with people she trusted, and in the end, she signed for it. She's not sure if she would make the same move today, but she did it then.

Now the group could really swing into action. They set up a schedule to ensure the bus was manned around the clock. They hung newspaper clippings in the mobile command unit so that newcomers could learn what was going on; they created an assembly-line letter writing campaign, and various committees met and discussed plans of action. As things came together, Cyndy, physically exhausted, began going home at night occasionally to sleep "in a real bed."

One of Cyndy's proudest moments was when Senator Connors visited the site. He told her, "When I first started getting letters, I was interested and understood the concern, but when they started bringing the letters in sacks, I realized something big was going on." He said he had never received so much mail over any one issue in all his time in office and commented that one big difference was the unusually large number of handwritten letters and personal notes.

"Normally when there is an issue like this, we get a petition or two, and petitions don't hold up—they're pretty much worthless," he said. "You guys are probably going to win this because of your letter writing efforts. Politicians don't know what the people are thinking unless they let them know, and they hear the people who are yelling the loudest."

Cyndy estimates that by the end of the campaign, they had mailed more than 50,000 letters.

***

On November 9, 1987, at a Jackson Township Committee meeting, Dan relayed Governor Kean's assurances that "radium-contaminated soil will never find a home at the Colliers Mills Wildlife Management Area." Kean had made the promise to Dan a week earlier, at a dedication ceremony for veterans, and given the mayor permission to quote him: "There's not a chance in a million the soil will be coming to Jackson Township."[27]

"I really appreciated hearing those words," Dan said. "It had been a tough year."

The DEP contracted with TFC Nuclear Associates to take 100 barrels from Montclair, process them with other radioactive dirt in Tennessee, and then ship them to a federally certified dump site in Washington State. Kean is said to have found it ironic that the soil had to be made more hazardous before it could be disposed of.[28]

Quadrex, of Oak Ridge, Tennessee, was awarded the contract for the remaining 4,900 barrels in Montclair, but a home still needed to be found for the 10,000 drums in Kearney. The DEP issued letters to all the state's municipalities asking if they would be willing to house the drums temporarily. Dan threw his in the garbage.[29] The remaining drums were eventually shipped to Envirocare, in Clive, Utah, for disposal at a licensed low-level radioactive facility.

On November 24, 1987, Senator Connors sent a letter to Dan, which read in part as follows:

> The events of recent months do not reflect well on the Department of Environmental Protection, but they do serve to illustrate the tremendous spirit and pride of the citizens and officials of Jackson Township. With each of you standing shoulder to shoulder, we were indeed capable of halting the outrageous DEP plan to store hazardous wastes in the Pinelands in the Colliers Mills Wildlife

Management Area. We were most proud to be at your side
in this tremendous challenge.[30]

The three arrests made on Saturday, June 6—the day the trucks
rolled in—were the only arrests made during the 6 months of tension
at Colliers Mills. No violence ever erupted, and no injuries were
reported.

Dan said, "It was exciting. I'm proud of the stand everyone took,
how everyone behaved, and proud of how it all ended up—that's the
great part."

"It was a long battle," Cyndy said, "but we won. I think the two
main reasons we won are, one, everyone stuck together no matter
what, and, two, we wrote thousands of letters. The politicians, the
DEP, and the Department of the Interior were bombarded with letters, and that's what, I think, really won it for us."

Dan and his wife, Vickie, smiled as they looked around their house,
all decked out for the Christmas holiday. "None of the doors has
closed right in this house since that day," Dan said, thinking back to
June 4, 1987, and the doors he and his brother were unloading when
he got word to call Senator Connors right away. "My brother put them
in the basement, which was damp, and I didn't get to go down there
for at least a month and a half. They all warped—so we get a reminder
of what happened that year every time we close the door."

Endnotes

1. Nanny Fröman, "Marie and Pierre Curie and the Discovery of Polonium
   and Radium," Nobelprize.org, December 1, 1996, nobelprize.org/nobel_
   prizes/physics/articles/curie/index.html (accessed December 24, 2007).
2. Ibid.

3. Denise Grady, "A Glow in the Dark, and a Lesson in Scientific Peril," *New York Times*, October 6, 1998, query.nytimes.com/gst/fullpage.html? sec=health&res=990DE1D61E38F935A35753C1A96E958260 (accessed December 24, 2007).

4. Mel Kaye, "Radium Dial Painting and Its Tragic Consequences," *NAWCC Bulletin*, April 2005, nawcc.org/pub/articles/apr05/apr05.htm (accessed December 24, 2007).

5. Grady, "A Glow in the Dark, and a Lesson in Scientific Peril."

6. Ibid.

7. Kaye, "Radium Dial Painting and Its Tragic Consequences."

8. Debbie Galant, "Living With a Radium Nightmare," *New York Times*, September 29, 1996.

9. U.S. Environmental Protection Agency, "Superfund," September 21, 2007, epa.gov/superfund/about.htm (accessed December 24, 2007).

10. Eckardt C. Beck, "The Love Canal Tragedy." *USEPA Journal*, January 1979, epa.gov/history/topics/lovecanal/01.htm (accessed December 24, 2007).

11. Department of Health and Human Services, Agency for Toxic Substances and Disease Registry, "Public Health Assessment: Montclair/West Orange Radium Site; Montclair/West Orange, Essex County, New Jersey," www.atsdr.cdc.gov/HAC/PHA/montclair/mon_p1.html (accessed January 4, 2009).

12. Correspondence from DEP Commissioner Richard T. Dewling, June 30, 1986.

13. Jay Johnston, "Jackson Site to Get Radium-Tainted Dirt," *Asbury Park Press*, June 5, 1987: A1.

14. "Temporary Storage of Radium. Contaminated Waste at McGuire Air Force Base," memorandum by NJ Pinelands Commission Executive Director Terrence D. Moore to Franklin E. Parker, Chairman of the Commission, October 15, 1985.

15. Johnston, "Jackson Site to Get Radium-Tainted Dirt."

16. Todd B. Bates and Kirk Moore, "Federal Officials Draw Criticism Over Missile Site," *Asbury Park Press*, June 10, 1987, A8.

17. New Jersey Department of Environmental Protection, Press Release No. 87/204, June 4, 1987.

18. John M. Giase, "Radon Decision Outages Officials in Ocean County," *Asbury Park Press*, June 5, 1987, A9.

19. Press Brick Township Bureau, "Mayor Urges Residents to Halt Radon Transport," *Asbury Park Press*, June 5, 1987, A9.

20. Joseph F. Sullivan, "Rally Protests the Storage of Tainted Soils," *New York Times*, June 5, 1987.

21. Ibid.

22. Patricia A. Mallow and Roberta Wells, "Jackson, Plumsted Residents Mobilize," *Asbury Park Press*, June 9, 1987, A2.

23. Bob McHugh, "Interior Head Opposes Radon Plan," *Ocean County Observer*, June 11, 1987, 1.

24. Jay Johnston, "Ex-Dep Chief Hired to Study Soil Storage," *Asbury Park Press*, June 16, 1987, A1.

25. "Statement of Assembly John T. Hendrickson, Jr. for the New Jersey Radium Radon Advisory Board Public Comment Period," July 1, 1987.

26. Office of the Governor, RadioWriter Legislative Alert No. 2162, June 15, 1987.

27. Patricia A. Mallow, "Mayor Assured About Tainted Soil," *Asbury Park Press*, November 10, 1987.

28. Alvin S. Felzenberg, *Governor Tom Kean: From the New Jersey Statehouse to the 9-11 Commission* (Piscataway, NJ: Rutgers University Press, 2006), 288.

29. Mallow, "Mayor Assured About Tainted Soil."

30. Senator Leonard T. Connors Jr. and Assemblyman Jeffrey W. Moran, personal correspondence to Mayor Daniel J. Black, November 24, 1987.

Hands-on History

Back in 1976, Niki Negus was a fresh-faced college junior. She got a job as a spinner and weaver at the Old Village at Smithville, which recreates a colonial settlement. Niki wore a cotton dress with billowing sleeves, complete with apron and a white scalloped bonnet covering her long brown hair.

The buildings were heated with wood, and every day resident decoy carver Gary Giberson would bring Niki cedar from his family's property to feed the fire. Gary wore a leather apron and knee-length stove leg pants, held up with suspenders. He had reddish-brown hair and a beard, with an Elmer Fudd-style corduroy cap on his head.

"He was a little smitten with me," Niki said with a smile. "He started courting me in costume. He brought me flowers from the gardens there and chocolate éclairs because he knew I loved them, and so we ended up getting married."

I could hardly wait to hear Gary's side of how they met. I admit I didn't expect his version to be quite as romantic as Niki's. I was wrong.

"She was the cutest little girl in there. She had the sweetest personality," Gary said. "So I kinda took a liking to her, and I would pick wildflowers for her. But what she didn't know," he grinned, "is that I would sneak in there early. I would move wedges in her loom so it wouldn't work, or I would make her spinning wheel lopsided so it wouldn't work.

"The only person in the whole village who could fix a spinning wheel or loom so it would work was me—so I would go over there and tip my hat and say 'Good morning, Miss Niki, I understand your loom isn't working.' She would say, 'Yes. I don't understand it. I left last night and it was fine.' I would tell her that they are made out of wood and they can warp overnight. Then I would cut out a quick wedge for her and fix it, and I was her hero."

Niki feigned surprise at this revelation. "And our marriage has been built on lies and deceit ever since," she said, her hazel eyes twinkling as she smiled lovingly at Gary.

The couple married in June 1978 and had three daughters, Amy, Megan, and Robin. Niki stayed home to raise the girls and tried to continue weaving and spinning. She was soon making baskets instead "because Amy decided she liked to play my loom like a harp. I put it away but decided I had to do something. One day, I was watching a television show on how to cut down a tree and make a basket, and I decided I could do that, so I taught myself.

"You basically just start with a product and do 'under,' 'over,' and weave it into a shape," Niki said as she demonstrated the technique. Her hands flew over the strips of reed, expertly weaving them into position. Over the next hour, she deftly created eight baskets, all the while talking with me.

"When my kids were little, we really couldn't afford to send them to preschool, so I made baskets and sold them, and that's how we paid the tuition," she told me.

Niki's workshop is warm and inviting, with numerous baskets hanging on either end of the bay window that overlooks the Giberson farm. Bookcases line both sides of the spacious room, with craft books and Gary's decoys filling the shelves. A framed picture proclaims, "Contentment is not the fulfillment of what you want, but the realization of how much you already have."

In the center of the room is a large table where Niki's students gather to learn basket making and other crafts. Niki makes most of her baskets with reed, often incorporating other materials, such as deer antler, into the design. "Reed comes from the bamboo family," she explained to me. "I've done wood, but can you imagine being halfway though a project and having to say, 'Can you cut me down another tree so I can finish this basket?'" She also uses vines from her garden.

In one corner of the room stands Niki's spinning wheel, one of several she owns. She doesn't just spin the wool—she is involved in the process from start to finish. Several hundred yards from where we sat was the enclosed 5-acre pen for her sheep. The Gibersons have had sheep since 1988.

"I have only one boy sheep and seven girl sheep," Niki said. "The boy is a Merino. Merino wool is kinda short and wavy. The girls are Lincoln-Cotswold crosses—their wool is long and not so wavy, so when I breed them, my goal is to get long, wavy wool.

"This is the boy. He's got horns and knows how to use them," she laughed, showing me a photograph of her sheep. "He's also been a very good dad; last year he produced 10 babies out of six girls—four sets of twins and two singles. His name is Merlin, since he's a magician." Niki explained that Merlin is a young ram, only 2 years old. "You should have only one ram on a farm—I have seven happy girls and one happy boy. The boys fight, and they would actually kill each other if they could. They're very territorial. They want their women, and that's it."

Niki explained that she feeds and waters the sheep every day. The fence, she said, is mainly to keep predators out, as opposed to keeping the sheep in. "Sheep are not very smart," she said, "and they are pretty happy here. They know they will be fed here."

Once a year in the spring, the sheep are sheared. Niki used to do it herself, but these days, in the interest of time, she hires someone who can shear a sheep in 10 minutes; she said it might take her an hour and a half. A good wool sheep can produce 16 pounds of wool.

The wool is then brushed and carded, which is the process of pulling the wool across a card to straighten out the fibers so they are lined up end to end for spinning. Back in colonial days, Niki explained, little girls would do the brushing and teasing, and then girls around the age of 12 would be responsible for carding the wool. The wool is washed either before or after carding, depending on personal preference. After carding, the wool product is called a *rolag* and is ready for spinning.

Niki demonstrated spinning to me, her foot pumping the pedal as her hands expertly fed the rolag into the wheel. Sheep's wool contains lanolin, which is very good for the skin; in fact, it is an ingredient in many hand creams. We laughed that it must be the secret recipe for Niki's youthful appearance.

Occasionally, Niki will dye the wool, using only natural dyes. "Black walnuts make a pretty brown dye; onion skins make a gold," she told me. "Back in colonial days, if you wore purple or red, people knew you were very wealthy because those [dyes] were hard to come by. When you think of royalty, you think of red or purple; those dyes were imported from the Orient."

The next step would be to either weave, knit, or crochet the wool. If you wove the fibers, the step after that would be to cut and sew the fabric.

Niki is involved in every aspect of the wool process, and sometimes that means being a sheep midwife. "When lambs are born, they are supposed to come out feet first, which makes sense if you think about it, because their shoulders are very narrow," she said. "If their head comes out first, they'll get jammed.

"Many times, what I see first is a nose or a tongue, and I have to put the head back and reach in and turn the lamb. The first time it happened, I called the woman I bought the sheep from and asked her what to do. She said, 'You know what to do, so just go in and do it,' and I said, 'OK, I just needed permission.'"

Watching Niki stroll around her farm, showing off her sheep, berries, and a beautiful grape arbor, you might assume she had been raised in the country. Niki actually hails from Princeton. "You could say I'm a Princeton Piney," she said with a laugh.

It all started when Niki enrolled in Stockton College, in Galloway Township, to become an animal behaviorist. She had trouble with calculus. "My brain doesn't work that way," she said. "Neither does mine," I told her, feeling glad to have at least one thing in common with this seemingly tireless sheep farmer, artisan, and instructor.

"So I left school for a year so I could figure out what I wanted to be when I grew up," Niki said. "I took an apprenticeship in spinning and weaving. I told the woman I went to that I'd really like to learn how to do this, and she said, 'Well, I'd like to teach you, but only if I like you. I'll give you one class. If we get along, you can come back; if not, then I really don't want to teach you.'

"I said that was fine, and she told me the class was $5. I was to come at 8:00 in the morning and stay until 8:00 at night. We ended up getting along really well; we drank a lot of tea together and figured out all the world's problems. She taught me to spin and weave and dye, and she was very good at all those things, so I was very fortunate."

Niki then returned to college and changed her major to early American crafts and culture, "never knowing in a million years what I was going to do with it," she said, laughing.

After the Gibersons married, they moved into the house where Gary had been born in the town of Port Republic, along the Mullica River. In 1986, Niki got a call from her uncle who said that her aunt was dying of cancer. Niki headed off to say goodbye and give her aunt permission to die. She packed up her three daughters, who were 2, 4, and 6 at the time, and brought them to her mother's house in Princeton.

Niki's aunt died before Niki arrived, so Niki helped her uncle with the funeral arrangements and then went back to her mother's to spend the night. About 2 AM, she got a call that their house back in Port Republic was on fire. The entire house was gutted from the fire, leaving only a shell and roof.

Immediately after the fire, all of the townspeople gathered together and gave Niki and her family all the things they would need to get started again. The people were so wonderful, Niki recalled. She told Gary at the time, "There is no way I can even things out, but we have to find a way to give something back." The insurance took 5 months to be settled, and the Gibersons rebuilt the house themselves over the next 3 years. They decided to add a classroom to one end and establish it as the Swan Bay Folk Art Center.

"So we ended up building this classroom with the idea that, yes, we would be charging money for [classes], but we would be teaching historical crafts, which is what we both knew how to do," Niki explained. "Our object was to help people feel good about themselves and to teach them to create their own history. We do all kinds of hands-on, historical things because people can come and go. If you leave stuff behind, people can say, 'Oh, my great-great-grandmother made this.' We really feel that is an important thing to do."

The Gibersons not only teach history, they live it. "Everything we do at some point was used for basic survival," Niki said. "Spinning the wool, knitting, weaving baskets—these are all things that had to be done in order for people to survive. We grow our own grapes and raspberries and make our own jelly. Next year's project is a more extensive jelly maker's garden."

The jellies and jams Niki makes are Jersey Fresh-certified, meaning that she uses only ingredients that she grows herself or purchases from other New Jersey farms. She prepares them in Buzby's commercial kitchen in Chatsworth, and R. Marilyn Schmidt proudly displays them on the shelves. "Marilyn has sold probably about 500 jars this year and is ordering more all the time," Niki exclaimed, adding, "She is amazing. She really is my hero.

"There is no way you can't believe in a God when you look at fruit and how good it tastes and how well the mixes go together and how pretty it looks in the jar," Niki said. She also pointed something out to me that I never realized before—all colors go together in nature in a perfect blend; nothing ever clashes. (I should probably try to enlist God's help the next time I try to redecorate my house!)

Niki holds Friday Friendship Nights, when women can come with some of their friends and learn a craft and unwind. For the younger set, she offers colonial tea parties and a project called the Create-a-Friend doll. Girls get to choose their doll's skin, eye, and hair color and hairstyle. Niki helps the girls stuff and assemble the dolls, after which they pick out an outfit and receive a birth certificate. Create-a-Friend doll making is a popular activity with the Girl Scouts and for birthday parties, Niki said.

A big believer in education, Niki is constantly teaching—both at the Swan Bay Folk Art Center and through Atlantic County Special Services in Mays Landing, where she serves as an aide for preschoolers 5 days a week.

"I always ask kids, 'What would you live without if you didn't have electricity?' One time, a little girl said, 'I wouldn't have a light in my refrigerator.' I said, 'Do you think you would have a refrigerator?' She said no. Then I ask, 'How would you get ice in July if you didn't have a freezer?' And they say, 'Well, you'd go to Alaska, you'd get a boat, and …' I stop them and tell them that they wouldn't have ice, that before there were freezers, there was no such thing as an ice cold drink in the summer.

"Just the fact that they wouldn't have a closet full of clothes amazed them," Niki continued. "I tell them that you had no choices—you had your Sunday outfit and your everyday outfit. They can't imagine life without a computer or a television.

"I tell them that in colonial days, your job was to help your family to survive. You would help with cooking, you would help with dishes, you would help with laundry, you would help with younger brothers and sisters—you would help with all those things that were necessary to help your family survive.

"Nowadays," she said sadly, "a child's job is to do well in school and keep busy without getting into trouble. Really, that's what it's about—it gives them lack of purpose. They try to fill their hours with things to do, like playing video games. My kids weren't allowed to play video games; I was the meanest mom in town."

Niki told me how her daughters wanted a trampoline, so she told them that they could give up TV for a year and earn it. During that year, the Gibersons had Friday night movies: They picked out a movie, and all watched it together. For the first 2 weeks after giving up TV, the girls went through withdrawal, but then they wandered outside and ended up building forts and "playing wilderness," which included Gary's teaching the girls how to track animal prints and find teaberries and other edible foods in the woods, as his grandfather had taught him. "After that year, they wanted to know if we could do it again. They did better in school, they read more, they played better together—they loved each other more. Today, we are just filling up hours of time and not giving kids a purpose."

***

Basket making is a functional art form that has been practiced by women in the Pine Barrens since colonial times. "If you needed to pick apples or carry laundry, you made a basket for it," Niki told me. "Today, however, more women are coming to the classes to make something I call 'clutter baskets.' It's more about storage and organization than practicality or decoration. We all lead busy lives, and we need places to stash what we don't have time for."

Niki described how spinning and weaving began in the colonies. "In the 1700s, England had laws saying that you were not permitted to bring looms, spinning wheels, or sheep into the colonies, because the King of England wanted the colonists to depend on English products. The English taxed glass; they even taxed needles. So once the people said, 'No more taxes! This is enough,' they had to learn to be self-sufficient. Which meant you didn't go to Macy's or Wal-Mart to buy your clothes; you had to make them yourself.

"As they spun wool, they would tell a tale or *spin a yarn*, and that's where that term came from. It became very important to make your own clothing; in some places, you could even pay your taxes in spun wool. Someone in every household knew how to spin and how to sew because you needed clothes to wear.

"It was a necessity—it had to be done, whether you lived in the Pine Barrens or Virginia or New England, unless you were very wealthy, and then you could pay someone else to do it. Without people becoming patriotic and saying we need to produce this stuff ourselves, we wouldn't have been independent in this country.

"Even though all these laws were written in Parliament, they weren't enforced very well, and people would sneak pieces of wood over on ships so that when they arrived here they could put them together as a loom or spinning wheel. There were itinerant weavers who would go all over in their wagons with their looms on the back because not every house had a loom to weave cloth on.

"The word *spinster* is not a negative word; it is a very patriotic term. When the woman did not get married, she spent her time spinning wool for her family. It was an important job that needed to be done. Here these women couldn't take the time to be courted. They were doing their patriotic duty, and it was looked on very highly, like men going off to war, which is kinda cool when you think about it."

Niki's goal is "to try every cool thing before I die." I asked her what the coolest thing she had done so far was, and she gave it serious thought before answering.

"I love making the jelly. I just love everything I do. It's really fun watching people create things, too—that's probably the coolest thing. Being able to help other people create things and express themselves. For example, a couple of my students are cancer patients right now. Two of them are making baskets for generations that are not born yet. It's really amazing to me that their legacy is going to live on through a basket—which might sound silly to a lot of people, but it's important for them to leave something because they might not make it, so they come here and do something creative. They feel good about themselves when they are done, and they're creating something for future generations. It's a lot of fun to watch that process happen.

"And a lot of talking goes on here. Women usually think through their mouth—men don't, but women do. One woman was in an abusive relationship, and she ended up leaving her husband because she was able to talk through things here.

"The funniest thing that ever happened here was that one of my friends, a good Christian woman, was coming to basket classes. Another woman would come [to the same classes] here week after week; she would just cry and cry because she wanted to have a baby so badly and wasn't getting pregnant. Through conversation, it came out that she wasn't married to the man she was trying to get pregnant with. She had been living with him for 7 years, so in her mind, she was married to the guy. So my friend says, 'You know, Maria, maybe if you got married, God would bless you and you would have your baby.' So she got married to the guy and got pregnant on the honeymoon!

"Just to be able to watch things like that happen, to be a small part of other people's lives, is amazing. I've had people coming here since 1988, and it's not because they need to know how to make a basket. They come for other reasons—they leave with a basket, but there are other things that happen in the mix, so I guess that's the coolest thing."

The Donkey and the Lantern

Canada geese were skimming effortlessly across the surface of Lake Meone in Smithville. It was a clear, spring-like day, and the sun glistened on the water. The birds moved toward the dock, where Gary Giberson was waiting to feed them.

Suddenly, the first goose stopped and raised its head as a distant sound grew louder. He stretched his neck upward and flapped his wings. The others became startled and began honking. The lead goose lifted off, and the others followed in formation.

A helicopter set down nearby. Gary—6 feet tall in his Florsheim leather boots—ran over, waving his arms. "You can't land here!" he shouted above the whirring of the chopper's blades.

The engine cut off, and the state police pilot climbed out and informed Gary that his passenger was then-New Jersey Governor Brendan T. Byrne. "You can land wherever you want," Gary said apologetically.

Byrne climbed out of the helicopter, surprised at the man's gumption. "Why are you so upset?" he asked.

"Because you scared my geese," Gary replied.

"What do you mean, *your* geese? Aren't they wild?" Byrne asked.

"Yeah," Gary admitted. "But I feed them every day and talk to them."

Byrne put his hands on his hips. "You talk to them? Let me hear you."

Gary asked if the governor wanted the geese to come back. "Sure," Byrne said skeptically. As Gary began to honk, the geese suddenly circled back to the spot on the water where they had been gliding minutes earlier.

Byrne was dumbfounded and asked Gary his name. When he replied that his name was Gary Giberson, the governor shook his head. "No, your name is 'Honker' Giberson," he said. "Would you like to have lunch with me and tell me how you learned to do all this?"

As it turned out, the governor was a friend of the proprietors of the Old Village at Smithville, Fred and Ethel Noyes, and often stopped by. That initial meeting was the beginning of a friendship between Gary and the governor that has spanned more than 30 years, during which Gary—resident decoy carver for the Old Village at Smithville—has produced numerous carvings for Byrne. "To this day, I still consider him my hero," Gary said.

As a boy, Gary learned the art of decoy carving from his grandfather. "My family had a sawmill, so I had wood to play with," he explained. "I would make birdhouses and put them together; I put 20 nails in one piece of wood and split it. Kids don't know better, but I eventually learned, and when I started making decoys, my grandfather was so proud of me.

"My grandfather called me *Dorothy* every day of my life," Gary said. "I was the original 'boy named Sue.'"

"Why would he call you Dorothy?" I asked with a raised eyebrow. As soon as the words came out of my mouth, I realized Gary had been waiting for the prompt.

"Because it would make me cuss," he said. "I was raised in a cussing family. I would say 'You old so-and-so,' and he would say, 'That's a good one, ... *Dorothy*' and reach into this little pocketbook he had. He would fish around and pick out a penny and give it to me. I learned to put five cusswords in a row and get a nickel."

Gary likes to tell stories like this as he demonstrates his skill at decoy carving. He boasted to us that he can hold his audience's attention for more than 2 hours as he carves.

Gary first started demonstrating his craft in 1962 at the Historic Town of Smithville. In 1974, the town was sold for $13 million to the American Broadcasting Company. Fred and Ethel Noyes had a summer theater there, and Gary made carvings for such luminaries of the stage and screen as Zero Mostel, Victor Borge, Ben Vereen, Ethel Merman, and Robert Young.

Later, on his own, he made carvings for comedian Jack Carter, *Sesame Street*'s Bob McGrath, radio personality Jean Shepherd, singer Connie Francis, and collectors Mr. and Mrs. David Schlapfer.

"I made a pair of hooded mergansers for Jimmy Stewart," Gary recalled. "He had come to see Congressman Bill Hughes, who was the head of patents. Stewart was lobbying him to vote against the colorization of old films. Hughes commissioned me to carve the ducks for Stewart.

"I got invited to talk with Stewart. I presented the decoys to him, and he wouldn't put them back in the box. Other people were giving him things like yearbooks from Princeton, because he graduated from there, and he was putting them to the side, but he wouldn't let go of my ducks. He had them on his lap in the limousine on the way to the airport, so I was really proud of them."

In 1978, Gary was invited to join Wheaton Village in Millville and accepted. Soon after, Governor Byrne called Smithville looking for Gary and was told he was now working at Wheaton. As Gary recalled, "He called Barry Taylor at Wheaton Village and said,

'President Carter is coming to make a presentation at NAFEC, and I want to give him something from an artist in New Jersey. I would like to have a Gary Giberson carving.'

"So it's 4:00 in the afternoon, and work is over for the day. We're sitting in there drinking a can of beer—I have an open can in my hand and beer on my breath, and here comes the big boss. So I slid the can behind something and tried not to talk at him. He said 'What do you have that we can give the president?' I thought he was joking around and started pointing to various carvings.

"He said, 'I'm serious. Governor Brendan Byrne just called me, and he wants you to do a carving for him.' So I had this carving I had started for Flora Maze—she was a glass artist in the village at the time—and I said, 'Flora Maze, I have a chance to do a presidential commission. I don't have anything started yet, and your bird is three-quarters done. Can I use it and make you another one?' She told me to go for it.

"So I got all the kids from the shops and said, 'Go to the library—I need a picture of a fiddler crab; You, get me an arrowhead plant.' I sent all these kids out, then called my wife on the phone and said, 'Niki, bring me my supper and my paint, I'm pulling an all-nighter. The kids are helping me; I'm doing a presidential commission.' So she comes with my supper and paints, and in walks a kid with two or three books with fiddler crab pictures in them, and another kid dug up an arrowhead plant for me and sets it down.

"President Carter's daughter, Amy, was 10 at the time, and I had seen a picture of her wearing this yellow dress to school. I started carving an arrowhead plant with a yellow flower with the leaves and all and put it alongside the driftwood. I finished carving the Greater Yellowlegs bird as I listened to bluegrass music. The fiddler crab was the bird's dinner. The kids all went home, and I finished at 8:00 in the morning.

"I signed it on the bottom, 'Presented to President Carter from Governor Brendan T. Byrne, carved by Gary Giberson.' Byrne sent his chauffeur to pick it up at 9:00, but I was so tired, I just left it there and went home. The next day, on the front page, column one, it read 'Carver's Creation in White House,' alongside a beautiful picture of the carving."

Gary recalled his first art show—in 1965 at the Cherry Hill Mall. "I had shorebirds tagged for $8 apiece and didn't sell anything, so I raised the price to $16 and sold three or four. Then I put $32 price tags on them and sold them all!" Today, Gary sells a pair for $1,200.

Gary demonstrated his skills for Andrew and me. Sitting on a specially made bench called a *schnitzelbunk*, he took a piece of sandpaper and folded it into thirds to keep the decoy from sliding as he worked. With his apron and corduroy duck hunter's cap, and with his small, wire-framed glasses perched on his nose, he was clearly slipping into character for us and enjoying every moment of it.

"I can carve a duck head and sand it and have it ready for painting in 15 minutes; people call me a liar, but I make money doing it," he told us as he cut. "I can really carve a head in 5 minutes and take another 5 minutes to sand it, so really it's 10 minutes, or used to be when I had more strength. Now it takes me about 15 to 20 minutes."

As he showed us how to transform a block of wood into a duck's head, Gary chewed on a piece of wood. As he cut the wood and ticked off the nine basic steps to creating the head, he occasionally slipped into "Piney talk," all the time watching to see if we noticed.

"I love to reach out to people and get into character and all; I'm sure I would have succeeded as an actor or maybe a lawyer, presenting a case," he said. "I've had so much fun with my life, and I've been so lucky reacting with people—just having fun with people. That's something I learned from my grandfather."

The Giberson family owns 6,800 acres of meadows near the Mullica River in Port Republic. Gary's grandfather, Alonzo

Giberson, and Alonzo's brothers were commercial fishermen. "All during the Depression, they would catch anywhere from $700 to $1,100 worth of rockfish a night," he said. "The cars would come in and out of my grandfather's driveway—he would give you some homemade butter, a piece of smoked bacon, and if you needed it, a $10 bill. So on Sunday, the cars would just pull in—everybody loved my grandfather. He was ornery, he was cantankerous; he'd buy a wagon for $5 and put $3 worth of paint on it and sell it for $30. He owned a sawmill, and he was a perfectionist when it came to sawing lumber."

Gary has some perfectionist tendencies himself when it comes to handcrafting, according to Niki. "He's taught me tons of things," she said. "Some of them broke my heart, but some of them were good. My mom was always very encouraging—she would say things such as 'Oh, it looks beautiful! It's handmade!' Gary would look at the same piece and say, 'You're going to leave that in there? That's a mistake.' I would shrug and say, 'Well, it's handmade.' Gary would correct me and tell me that just because it's handmade doesn't mean you can't do it right. I would be so sad that he wasn't telling me it was beautiful, but because of that, I became a better craftsperson."

"When I draw my patterns," Gary said, "I use the characteristics of each individual species." He pointed to the different decoys in his shop. "When I see canvasbacks on the water, they are regal. They look like the king sitting on the water, so I pull the head back, I blow the breast out, and I give them this stiff-shouldered, look-at-me! look.

"Mergansers are fast; they have these hairlike feathers on the back of the head. They look like they need a hairdresser. I make them look angry by carving a line over the eyebrow.

"Buffleheads—they have '*aww*-ability'—they're small and cute. The little ruddy duck is the smallest of all ducks. He has puffy cheeks and a real wide bill. Birds that have '*aww*-ability' make people reach for their wallet or pocketbook; they sell immediately."

Gary explained to us that all carving is basically rounding off the corners. Because he and Niki are firm believers in educating people about the history of their crafts, he gladly told Andrew and me about decoys.

"The decoy became very collectible; it is a very unique form of folk art," he said. "American Indians were the first ones to use decoys. They found out if you put lures on the water, the flying birds would see them and decide to come down to join them, feed with them, or rest with them, so the decoys worked.

"I found out that ducks can interpret color. If we look at a tree, we see three or four shades of green. Ducks look at a tree and see not only greens but blues, oranges, and reds; they can really interpret color. So color is very important to the decoy. When I found out what a duck actually sees, I became more interested in the color. The color of decoys changes with the seasons—they're in a breeding plumage in the spring; in the winter, they are a different color; in the fall, it changes again. Since we shoot at them in the fall, I try to paint them in a fall plumage."

Positioning is also important, Gary reminded us. Hunters are not allowed to bait the ducks with corn or any other food. Gary decided to create decoys that resemble ducks in a feeding frenzy. "So what I do is make my decoys look like they are over corn—their wings are loose, they're showing that beautiful color spectrum on their scalloper feathers, and their heads are high. I position them so that they are looking down; if a duck is sitting on the water with its head up, that's a sign that it is wary. If you point the bill down, it looks like the duck is over food or getting ready to dive or tip up—some ducks tip up, and some dive for food. When flying ducks see my personal decoys, they come at them, not over them. I have to be really careful because they get so low that I could shoot into my decoys.

"Decoys are unique in South Jersey because they are made hollow. The decoy is made in three pieces; the body is made in two halves, and then it is hollowed and joined together. A lot of places make hollow decoys, but New Jersey was the first. This made the decoy lighter and more buoyant, so it would float higher out of the water and have more lifelike movement on the water. Decoys must look contented. On opening day, ducks will come into clumps of mud, but after they have been shot at a few times, they're really wary, and it takes better decoys to become successful."

One thing Gary is emphatic about—and he says he has gotten into fights with other carvers over it—is that keels don't belong on decoys. "Keels belong on model sailboats," he told us. "When you put them on a decoy, they make them go straight, and there is no natural movement."

Gary showed us around his workshop area and his impressive collection of tools. Each of his pieces is more beautiful than the next, and the detail is amazing. In the center of the shop sits a raccoon family climbing a tree, made out of driftwood. Curiosity shows on the faces of the young coons as they scale the top branches.

"I learned a real cool lesson from this," Niki tells us as she points to the raccoon piece named *Action Reaction*.

"We were working for Fred Noyes at the time," she said. "Anything Gary carved, Fred would buy off of him, but Gary pretty much gave it away. We were earning only $240 a week between the two of us, and we never really had enough money to pay our bills.

"We needed $2,500 to pay our taxes, so Gary said to sell this piece for whatever I could get for it. I told Fred it was $5,000, and he told me that he never paid that much before and would have to think about it. The next day, he told me that he would give us $2,500 in cash and the rest in furniture that was worth about $2,500. There was a marble top table, a canopy crib, a rug—we made out really well. When Fred died, he willed all his carvings back to us, tax free, so we got this back, along with all the other carvings Gary had sold him over the years.

"So I learned a very good lesson from this: When you sell something like this, the money is gone, and the piece is gone, and then you have nothing. I'll never sell something like this again—I'll get another job first because there is no way he is ever going to produce anything like this again."

Gary collects classic cars and has built a 1930s-style gasoline station—much of it furnished with "treasures" he found on eBay—alongside his driveway. He is also proud of his family's heritage, which he happily shared with us.

"The Gibersons came here in 1637 and settled in Chestnut Neck, 3 miles from here up the road. They were Dutch, and their name was spelled *Geversen*. In 1680, the English said, 'New Jersey belongs to us, and you will swear allegiance to the king or we will deport you.' We didn't care who we swore allegiance to, so we said, 'OK, sign us up with King Charles II.'

"So they changed the spelling of our name from *Geversen* to *Giberson*—from a squarehead to a limey—so we're English now. During the Revolutionary War, there was a big battle here. Privateering was allowed; anyone who had a boat could go out and plunder the British ships. Privateers used all kinds of lures to draw the British ships onto the beach or onto a sandbar.

"One of the stories my grandfather told—that was passed down to him—the privateers took a donkey, and they tied a pole onto his foot and his shoulder. About 10 to 15 feet off the ground, they put a lantern, and they walked the donkey along the shoreline. Well, the lamp would move and go up and down. Any ship at sea would follow another ship at night, especially if the other ship was on the coastal side. So the privateers would start the donkey right near the water and just keep walking him inland a bit, and a ship would follow him in and run aground. Then the privateers would go out and surround the boat and get their stuff."

There is a lantern in Gary's life that he follows, and that is God. On a card on the windshield of his 1931 Model A Deluxe Roadster is verse 4 from Psalm 37: "Delight thyself in the Lord and you will receive the treasures of your own heart." The roadster's license plate reads PSM37.

Gary says he grows spiritually in the Lord every day; he put the scripture on his car so people will know he has put God into what he does. He says what the verse means to him is that "if I put God first in my heart, in my mind, and my soul, I can receive the treasures of my heart and enjoy them."

He continues, "I have a wonderful Christian family all around me, and I know I will probably do a carving demonstration or two when I get to heaven. It is such a unique feeling to know this is all vapor. One day my kids were on the floor playing, and the next day they were asking me for the keys to my car. Life is like a vapor, it goes so fast. I thought I would turn into my father, but I looked into my mirror, and I was my *grand*father."

Gary also has a deep passion for the Mullica River area. He spoke about the Atlantic white cedar that his family has made a living off for decades.

"On the north side, it is known as bog cedar. There's a lot of sandstone, and there are more iron deposits in the bog cedar. On the south side of the Mullica River is muck cedar—really rich cedar. It has a different color to it; it's whiter and clearer, and it even has a different smell and a different taste to it. I can tell whether the trees came from the north or the south side of the river—my grandfather taught me that.

"Atlantic white cedar grows like a stalk of celery—all the limb growth is on the top third of the tree. The bottom two-thirds of the tree are bare: no limbs, no knots—just beautiful, perfect, straight-grain wood. It is used for planking boats, for siding, and for shingles because it can be split easily."

Before Andrew and I left the Gibersons, I asked Gary if there was anything he wanted people to remember about the Pinelands. Without missing a beat, he replied, "I want them to come down and put a piece of pine needle in their mouth; I want them to come down and experience it. I don't want them to read it in a book some liberal has written; I can't stand what's happening with the people in North Jersey. They are in love with the Pines; they want to control it—control my life, control land that's been in my family for all these years. I am dead set against the [NJ] Pinelands Commission; I think the towns can run their own. Some towns are forced to be a big-growth area; we're lucky, because we're a low-growth area. We have no sewers and no water, so we have our own wells and our own septic system in the town, and you need a 1-acre lot to build on.

"I have 80 acres on this side of the road, and I can't build on it because it is in the Pinelands. I can't build on my own property for my own family. I got someone from North Jersey telling me this. I have someone from North Jersey telling me I can't feed my sheep this way, I have to do this with my garbage, I can't feed the birds because the black bears are here.

"The black bear that comes to my property is a dead black bear because I am a sheep farmer, and the coyote that comes onto my property is a dead coyote. We have all these animal-lover people who don't live in South Jersey; these bears and coyotes don't belong in South Jersey—that's what I want the people who come to the Pinelands to realize. This is a unique part of the country where we are, on this beautiful Mullica River, and we know how to preserve it ourselves."

Because he has been friends for years with former Governor Byrne who developed much of the Pinelands legislation, I asked Gary how he reconciles this friendship and his feelings.

"I would tell him, Brendan, it was a good idea in the beginning," Gary started, "but I think they should have compassion for landowners and families like ours. There are a lot of people who are influenced by developers, so maybe we do need the Pinelands Commission to control this, but they should have compassion. I don't develop my land for the sake of development. I want to develop it for my family to live on.

"This is what I'd like to do with the Pinelands: Get the developers with honest intentions and the Pinelands Commission together and say, 'Hey, there is a solution here.' The Pinelands Commission's directive is to say 'No, no, no,' and times are changing. You can't say 'no'; we ought to be able to say, 'Let's look at it, maybe there's a way.' If they would just say 'maybe,' instead of 'no.'"

Buzby's and The Cheshire Cat

Like the women in Niki Giberson's basketry group, the menfolk of the Pine Barrens like to gather to talk about the latest happenings. For many years, the meeting place of choice was the Chatsworth General Store, now known as Buzby's. In the early to mid-1900s, the men would come into the store to buy their shotgun shells or tobacco and sit for a while on the oak plank next to the penny candy counter, catching up on the latest news. It was on this plank that John McPhee sat and listened to the locals, gathering stories and inspiration for his classic book *The Pine Barrens*.

In the book, McPhee narrated the pattern of traffic in and out of the store, describing the manner of dress, conversations, and items purchased. One can easily visualize him sitting on the plank bench, taking careful notes. He described his initial observations:

> When I first stopped in there, I noticed on its shelves the usual run of cold cuts, canned foods, soft drinks, crackers, cookies, cereals, and sardines, and also Remington

twelve-gauge shotgun shells, Slipknot friction tape, Varsity gasket cement, Railroad Mills sweet snuff, and StateWide well restorer. Wrapping string unwound from a spool on a wall shelf and ran through eyelets across the ceiling and down to a wooden counter. A glass counter top next to the wooden one had been rubbed cloudy by hundreds of thousands of coins and pop bottles, and in the case beneath it were twenty-two rectangular glass dishes, each holding a different kind of penny candy.[1]

R. Marilyn Schmidt, the current owner of the store, has corresponded with McPhee. "He told me there used to be a radiator by these windows with a big oak plank. Everyone would sit there and solve the problems of the world, and he would join them and drink coffee. That's when he got interested in the Pines; he was only in his 20s when he wrote *The Pine Barrens*. This is where everyone met."

But this meeting place in a town dubbed the Capital of the Pines almost faded into oblivion. From 1990 to 1998, the store was vacant and its future uncertain. Only a handful of items—a few chairs, tables, and the candy counter with its penny candy glass dishes—remained in the dust. A tax lien and abandoned gasoline tanks from a former Esso gas station out front discouraged would-be purchasers.

It wasn't until Marilyn, a former tax assessor living in Barnegat Light, entered the picture that the store's future was secured. Marilyn knew how to acquire clear title, which involved purchasing the assignment of the tax lien and foreclosing on four owners and two banks.

"People thought I was buying a pig in a poke," she said, but her research into old tax maps proved she knew what she was doing. It had been widely assumed that the gasoline tanks were on the store's property, as most deeds ended their property line at the road's center, but every map she studied showed the boundary line ending at the front porch. A survey she ordered proved her right. Still, it took almost 2 years to gain clear title.

A week after she obtained the title, a fire broke out. "We had nailed the doors of the store closed when I was in the process of getting clear title, so the kids couldn't get in," she explained. "They had been drinking and smoking, and when they couldn't get in, they went in the barn with their cigarettes and burned that down. The fire spread to the outhouse and store.

"Fortunately, Buzby's was saved because it had asbestos siding on it. The firemen poured water on the building to save it and just let the barn burn. A lot of fire companies came out, and they all take credit for saving Buzby's. I wasn't here at the time, but my neighbor across the street—Bob Griffin—heard something he said sounded like bullets. He looked out and saw the flames and called the fire department. So in my eyes, he's really the one [who] gets the credit for saving the building. I was very fortunate."

She then began the painstaking and expensive task of restoring the building as closely as possible to its original condition. "We took down the other barn that was collapsing and kept all the white cedar siding from it. We used it to rebuild the outhouse on its original platform, and I use it as a tool shed."

To restore the building as accurately as possible, Marilyn researched its roots. She later used this information to file for the building's placement on both the state and national historic registers. It was accepted for the state register in 2002 or 2003 and was granted national status on April 21, 2004.

As part of the application process to get Buzby's on the U.S. Department of the Interior's National Register of Historic Places, Marilyn needed to provide a comprehensive history of Buzby's, which she wrote by drawing on her background as a technical writer and her years of researching and writing about various aspects of the Pines.

After she graciously agreed to share it with me, I stepped onto the restored wooden porch and back into time:

> The land that encompasses Chatsworth was part of the estate of Joseph D. Beers, a New York broker and a major investor in Pine Barrens property. Chatsworth, known as Shamong Station or Shamong until 1896, was a railroad town. The Raritan and Delaware Bay Railroad (R&DB) served the area from the early 1860s until the mid 1960s. With the line through Shamong Station completed in 1862, during the Civil War, one of the main sources of early revenue for the R&DB was to carry Union troops between New York City and Philadelphia.
>
> Then, with the end of the Civil War in 1865, Ocean County experienced something of an economic boom. Many local sea captains who normally engaged in the coastal trade had amassed large sums ferrying war materials in the Chesapeake Bay and the Potomac and James Rivers. Some of this money was now channeled into banking, real estate development, and local industry in Burlington and Ocean Counties. One result was an increased population in the area and demand for a new general store.
>
> Benjamin O. Wade obtained title to approximately one acre on the southwest corner of First Street and Main Street (now County Road 563). Wade had the present general store and residence built for him in 1865, and he weathered the changing fortunes of the community and the railroad, running the store for the next thirty-two years.[2]

Wade sold the building to Willis Jefferson Buzby in 1897. Willis and his wife Elisa "Myrtle" Buzby operated the store and lived in the residence upstairs. Mail service was provided by train until 1914, when a post office was established in Buzby's General Store. Myrtle served as the postmistress until her death. The post office moved to Prince Street in 1934 and later to its current location on Second Street.

In his book *Forgotten Towns of Southern New Jersey*, Henry Charlton Beck wrote that "the real power of the township is Willis Buzby, 'King of the Pineys,' who with his son, Jack, operates a combination store, service station and garage in Chatsworth." Beck went on to say that Willis had "ready advice on law, etiquette, investments, medicine and religion."[3]

Marilyn's history continues:

> The 1920s brought many changes to Chatsworth. The Buzbys owned one of the first telephones in Chatsworth, which aided many in the community. The increasing popularity of the automobile and subsequently improved roads created a need for gasoline. In 1921, the Buzbys were selling gasoline—Esso—to their customers, which included the local school system for its buses. Eventually there were three Esso pumps on the sidewalk in front of the store.
>
> In the late 1920s excursion trains brought people to the Chatsworth club and the area once again prospered. The roads were paved in 1930 and electricity was brought to Chatsworth and the store electrified in 1932.
>
> Buzby's General Store had no competition for a ten mile radius. Although for a time there was another store in Chatsworth, customers continued to travel from Hog Wallow, Speedwell, Friendship, Jones Mill, and other local places in the Pine Barrens to shop at Buzby's.
>
> Records indicate the store was remodeled around 1921 and again around 1935. The front (northwest) angled corner

door was added and large front windows installed. A prominent candy counter graced the east window area. The one-story rear addition, added sometime prior to 1900, used initially for storage of animal feed, was called the "Feed Room."

The property contained other buildings: a garage/workshop/barn, a barn, an outhouse, and an ice house. According to the late Katie Buzby, ice was cut from the Chatsworth Lake in the winter and stored in the ice house for summer use. Residents today continue to remark that Buzby's outhouse, a two-holer, was one of the cleanest in town and a white lace curtain always graced the window.

The period 1929 to 1940 saw the country in the Great Depression. People in the Pine Barrens were not affected to the extent of those in the cities. Those living in the Pine Barrens, the "Pineys," were used to living off their land; their gardens provided fruits and vegetables, which they preserved by canning, while hunting for deer, rabbits, ducks and other animals provided meat.

There was an annual cycle of seasonal activities and short-term employments that allowed traditional Pine Barrens residents to achieve a livelihood in the absence of steady full-time jobs. Flour, sugar, coffee, tea, and clothing were the main products they purchased. For these necessities, they depended on Buzby's.

Buzby's store was responsible for the survival of more than one Pine Barrens family. Some debts were paid, some not. The Buzbys were revered by the local citizenry. The store was not only their source of foodstuffs and necessities of life, but it was also the social and communication center of the Pine Barrens. It was one of the few general stores in the vast Pine Barrens.[4]

After the death of Willis on January 4, 1939, Myrtle deeded the property to their son, Willis Jonathan Buzby, who was known as Jack. Jack also inherited his father's title, as he and his wife, Katherine "Katie" Ritzendollar, were soon being called "King and Queen of the Pineys." The title may have been a variation on the one bestowed on William Torrey, often referred to as "King of the Pines" for his role in developing the R&DB. The railroad allowed Torrey to ship his charcoal and played an important part in the growth of Chatsworth's economy.

Many Chatsworth residents still recall the trains that ran through the town, and quite a few people have memories of Jack and Katie Buzby, as well. Everett Applegate, an author who was born and raised in Chatsworth, described his memories:

> Some of my fondest childhood memories were centered around Buzby's General Store. Willis Jonathan Buzby, if he could have stood up straight, would have been about five-foot eight-inches tall. Unfortunately, he was born with a left arm and leg that drooped in a strange manner, as did the left side of his face. As a result, his left side failed to harmonize with the right, and it gave his entire body a distinctive tilt.
>
> Local residents report that he was born prematurely and was so small that he fit into a cigar box lined with cotton. He kept this cigar box on a shelf in the store with a picture of himself as a newborn infant, and proudly showed them to anyone upon request. Fascinated that a newborn could be so small, I looked at that box and picture almost every time I went into the store.
>
> Jack, as everyone called Buzby, could still work very hard, but couldn't grasp things very well with his weak left arm. Instead, he would place something under that

appendage with his good arm to carry it around, leaving his right arm free for other tasks. He had a long wooden pole with a metal claw on one end that could be closed by squeezing a lever on the other end. He'd clamp onto objects he wanted to retrieve from high shelves. That claw, which was virtually another arm, was never far away from him.

He let me move toilet paper down from the top shelf using the contraption. But the claw had a flaw. It was not very efficient for lifting heavy cans of fruit or tomatoes. More than a few times, we dropped cans on the floor or on ourselves, but at my very young age, the claw seemed like the greatest of inventions.

Kate was a small, bird-like woman, and although very kind, she did not take guff from anyone. She had the ability to keep man, woman and child in line with just a stern glance. Although I didn't get paid, Jack and Katie allowed me to work in the store for all the potato chips, soda, and penny candy I wanted.

I pumped gas, filled cans of kerosene from a hand-cranked pump, stocked shelves, took out the trash, and did anything else they wished. I just loved to be around them, and felt they loved me as well. Kate called me Evie, short for Everett, and was just like a mother to me. I eventually moved onto other jobs around town, but only because I needed a real one that paid real money.[5]

Jeff Brower recalled that Buzby's was the first place in town to have a color television, which was kept in the window. "We just sat outside and said, wow!" Jeff said.

As Marilyn worked to restore the building, local residents would often stop by to see how it was going. They shared their memories of Jack and Katie and their affection for Buzby's store, pointing to various items and places in the old building and reminiscing. Their stories set the tone for the application to the National Register of Historic Places that Marilyn later completed. Part of her application reads as follows:

> Jack had been born in one of the rooms above the store. He married the girl next door, Katie Ritzendollar, and as a wedding gift they received the house across the street from the store. This had been Katie's grandmother's house. Jack and Katie had one daughter, Theresa. Together Jack and Katie ran the store serving the local community. Jack traveled weekly by rail to Philadelphia for supplies to satisfy the needs of the local citizenry.
>
> After World War II, the store remained the lifeline, social center, and communication center for many Pine Barrens residents. Buzby's was the source of information for a great area. When blueberry and cranberry farms expanded after the war, the busing of migrant workers into the area from as far away as Philadelphia began. Unemployed men, women, and even children were gathered by a padrone—a leader—who usually owned a bus and transported them to the blueberry and cranberry farms to work. A stop at Buzby's store was always a necessity before returning to Philadelphia.
>
> In the 1960s, hunting was a popular activity, not for sport per se, but for food. Buzby's supplied the gunning/hunting clubs with shotgun shells in addition to providing foodstuffs for the club. The store also served as a weigh station for the deer catch. It truly was the heart of the Pine Barrens.
>
> Others lived off the land cutting cordwood, gathering pine cones, ground pine, laurel, and holly for shipment to

the cities. Hunting provided meat and gardens their fruits and vegetables. At one time, Chatsworth had two general stores, three saw mills, two hotels, a railroad station, and many homes.

Jack and Katie continued to run the store until Jack's health failed. Then they retired to the house across the street. When Jack retired in 1966, local residents Albert and Margaret Scheiss purchased the store and continued to operate it until 1973. They then sold it to Robert and Kathleen DePetris who ran the store from 1973 to 1976. The store was then sold to a group—Gedeminas K. and Frances R. Gudaskus, et al.—which owned the store until 1983 when it was purchased by Thomas and Charlotte Hedges, et al. In 1986, they sold it to a family consisting of Joseph, Mary, Michael, and Maryellen Triano, who operated it for a few years and then leased it to Richard and Sarah Conrad, who operated it until 1990. The Conrads wished to purchase the store but were unable to come to agreement with the owners. The Conrads then closed the store and auctioned off the furnishings. Over the years, the store was often referred to as the "John Wanamaker's of Chatsworth."[6]

In 1996, Marilyn's company, Barnegat Light Press, Inc., purchased the tax lien assignment from GTL Investors (Breen Corp.) of Bordentown, New Jersey. Through Barnegat Light Press, Inc., and its Pine Barrens Press division, Marilyn has published more than 40 cookbooks, guides, and booklets.

Today, Marilyn considers the store a Pinelands resource center because, in her words, "it is the one place you can go to get everything related to the Pines. There really isn't any place else that sells these materials. As of this year, we have homemade jams and jellies made right here in my commercial kitchen, and they have proven very successful."

Those jams and jellies are made fresh by Niki Giberson of Port Republic and preserved under the label Swan Bay. The commercial kitchen was one of the upgrades Marilyn made to the original store. When she opened it in 1999, half the building on the first floor housed a café and the other half The Cheshire Cat gift shop.

"There really isn't any place around here [anymore] where you can get a cup of coffee and a sandwich, except when Robyn is open to get a hot dog."

Robyn is Robyn Bednar, whose hot dog stand across the street from Buzby's is open spring through fall. She started the stand on her father's [Bob Griffin's] property in 1989 as a way to earn money to pay for her tuition at Davis & Elkins College in West Virginia.[7] Joe Triano, owner of Buzby's at the time, tried to have Robyn closed down, contending that she did not seek a necessary site plan approval and certain variances before opening the stand. Robyn's attorney asserted this was not necessary, stating, "It's not laid in the ground; it doesn't have any utilities. Mr. Griffin rolls it out like a wheelbarrow in the morning, and rolls it back here at night."[8]

Joe Triano's main concern was competition, Robyn said. "The Trianos also said the stand cooled off business at their store, which they depend on as their sole source of income."[9]

Robyn made an effort to work things out with Triano, believing their businesses could complement each other and that cross-referral could help them both grow. Triano didn't see it the same way, however, and the case went all the way to the New Jersey Superior Court. Eventually, Robyn won, and soon after, Triano closed the store and moved to Florida. The whole thing cost both parties thousands of dollars and was newspaper fodder for the 3 years the case dragged on, with reporters dubbing it "the wiener wars."

Apart from the kitchen, Marilyn tried to stay true to the building's original design, with a few modern upgrades, including a handicap-accessible ramp and bathroom and an energy-efficient geothermal heating and air-conditioning system.

Marilyn interviewed several contractors before settling on Albert Morison, whose parents live next door to Buzby's to this day. "I think we met three times and decided to go ahead. We looked each other in the eyes and shook hands; we never had a thing on a piece of paper, and we're still good friends. That's hard to say with builders.

"He and I agreed on everything in the restoration here except the molding for the back hall. I wanted vinyl cove molding because it's a hard floor and it would be wet mopped. He didn't agree; he felt we should have a wood molding because it would look better for the store. We went on and on, and finally he said, 'I'll fix it.' I came back one day, and here's my wood molding with vinyl cove molding on top of it! So we both got our way, and that was our only disagreement."

Albert wasn't the only treasure Marilyn discovered through Buzby's. The store yielded lots of surprises as they removed the debris. The first thing they did was cart away 33 dumpsters' worth of trash.

Marilyn described some of the work that was necessary. "There were two barns—one burned and had to be cleaned up, and the other was dismantled. We had to clean the upstairs. There were layers of shag carpeting, beer bottles—you can't imagine the mess; it was unbelievable. There were holes in the floor—you had to watch where you went, or you would go right through. The upstairs bathroom floor had fallen down on the front hall below.

"The walls were paneled with dark plywood; we pulled all that off, and the original plaster was underneath, and you could still see the original moldings. We sanded the front hall floor; it turned out to be maple. Upstairs were the original footwide pine floorboards from 1865.

"Buzby's had been the main supplier of kerosene for the Pines," Marilyn said, recalling the 55-gallon cans that had been left behind in the basement. "There had been an outside entrance to the basement at one time, but it had been sealed with concrete, so the only way to get them out was to cut a hole in the floor because the stairwell was too narrow to bring them up. ... That was quite a chore. The floor was in bad condition and had to be replaced anyway, so it didn't much matter. We tore up the old oak floor and had a new pine floor put down.

"We found an old wooden molasses barrel pump, which is probably one of the oldest items here. It was a wooden barrel pump that was put in a barrel and molasses flowed out; it's a very fine old piece of work. They used molasses because years ago sugar was very expensive."

Outside Buzby's, as you faced the entrance, the exterior to the right was covered with aluminum. On the inside was pegboard. "I thought it was the ugliest thing in the world," Marilyn exclaimed. "I said to the builder, 'We have to get rid of it.'"

"Now wait a minute," Albert told her. He took out his claw hammer and popped off all the pegboard. Underneath was the original bay window—hidden away all those years! So they cleaned up the window and replaced the glass, and today it sits proudly as the focal point of the store.

Marilyn keeps an artificial Christmas tree in the window year round. She decorates it for the different seasons, putting sunflowers on it in the summer and, of course, lights during the winter holidays. "When it's lit up, you can see it as you come into town," Marilyn said. "It serves as a beacon to downtown Chatsworth." She also puts candles in all the windows throughout December, keeping them lit from dusk to dawn.

The fireplace was another great find. "It was bricked solid and painted fire-engine red when I got the store, and it was just ugly," said Marilyn. "So I had some masons come in. ... They chipped out all the new brick and told me that the original bricks underneath were hand-made and field-dried. You can see animal footprints, mainly raccoon, that walked on them while they were drying in the field. After much research, I found the appropriate mantel and had it put on. If the day comes when I have the money, I'll have the chimneys restored so I can have a fire in there. But that's an expensive chore, so it's on the long list of things to do in the future."

The outside porch was concrete and brick when Marilyn took over, but as it was originally wood, she and Albert decided to rebuild it. According to Marilyn, Albert insisted on mahogany so it would last for another hundred years. "And we have bronze boat nails in there because stainless steel would show up—everything was done just right. It was sort of Albert's monument; he was very proud of his job here, and rightly so."

Almost as an afterthought, Marilyn asked me if she had mentioned about getting her wells shot. No, I said, dumbfounded, I hadn't heard the story about the wells. She was more than happy to oblige.

"We didn't have running water, and with the men working and the fire concerns, we had to have water," she began. "So Albert said, 'Get Toppy to shoot your well,' and I called him to come out. I wasn't around when Toppy came by, and all of sudden, I see him come out of the cellar with a shotgun. I said, 'Toppy, you've got a gun!' and he matter-of-factly said, 'Yeah, I shot your wells. They work fine now.'

"I didn't know what to say. I thought *shooting the wells* was an expression for something they did; I didn't expect him to actually come here with a gun and shoot them. So I wouldn't let anyone touch the water until I had it tested; they all looked at me like I was crazy—nobody was worried about it but me, and of course it was fine, and the wells have worked ever since. Apparently when you shoot down into the wells, it loosens up the corrosion."

Books are probably Marilyn's greatest love, along with a "super-sized" cat named Pumpkin. "In doing my research for the historic register, I found out that both of the Buzby families [who] ran the store had a big orange cat that sat on the counter with them. His name was Billy. And I moved here with a big orange cat named Pumpkin ... and today he runs the store. He is also probably the most photographed cat in the United States. He loves it; he'll pose for you.

"And in the store, he has more visitors than I do. Customers meet him once, and everybody comes back to see Pumpkin. So he's good for business. He is 17 years old and doing very well for his age. He's an exceptionally large cat. I've only had two cats in my adulthood, and I didn't know the average cat weighs 7 to 8 pounds. Pumpkin weighs 27, so I just tell people he came supersized. He was named Pumpkin for color, but he grew into his name.

"He catches bats, he catches mice—he is very good at that—and brings them to bed usually. I am very good at getting rid of live and dead critters. Bats bothered me at first, but I got used to them; we have an attic full of them. We tried everything to get rid of them, but bats seem to prefer it here."

One of Marilyn's favorite books is *Alice in Wonderland*, by Lewis Carroll. She has an early edition with the original plates. When she first opened and Buzby's was divided between the café and the retail store, she named the shop portion The Cheshire Cat, after the character from *Alice in Wonderland*, because, as she said, "Sometimes I'd open and sometimes I wouldn't, sometimes I'm here and sometimes I'm not." She smiled. "You have to be familiar with the book to get that. ... I found out I needed to have regular hours, but I kept the name."

Marilyn is a spry lady with an inquisitive mind and a great sense of humor. She's worked as a biochemist, pharmacologist, and certified tax assessor. She has a real estate license and runs the store part-time, along with her publishing enterprise. I've known her for years, and apparently everybody else in the Pine Barrens has, too; it seems as if everyone I talked to brought up her name in conversation. Just like her predecessors, she has become a central fixture in the Pines. And although she is not a native, the townsfolk have welcomed her as one of their own.

"When they diagnosed my brain tumor, they scheduled surgery for the latter part of that week, so I didn't have time to tell anybody," she said. "I called my brother and said 'I will be in the hospital for a while.' I was sort of blah and emotionless, which was due to the tumor. The next day, I was locking up, and my builder's father went by in his motorized cart, as he has multiple sclerosis. I said, 'Al, I'll be away for a few days. I'm going in the hospital. I have a brain tumor.' He told me he would pray for me. I never had a chance to tell anyone else because I was going in the hospital the next morning and we had to leave here at 3:00 or 4:00 in the morning.

"My brother, Ed, would come by and feed Pumpkin. The pattern of lights was different in my house, and the neighbors knew something was wrong. They were all so upset—they were calling my brother and stopping by, and he didn't know who any of these people were.

"When I got home, I had 800 emails to go through. I was back working in 2 weeks, which I thought was pretty good. People kept coming by to see how I was doing; they were very concerned. Steve Lee—the cranberry farmer down the road—was so upset. He learned about it at a Pinelands Commission meeting, and he drove by and saw the lights on. He came to a screeching halt and came running in and said, 'I didn't know you had trouble—anything we can do?' He can't do enough for you; the Lees are gentlemen to the umpteenth degree. I said, 'No, everything is fine. It's all under control,' but he felt so bad that he hadn't known. Betty Wilson, who was head of the Commission, must have stopped here also—she wrote me a very lovely note wishing me well.

"I can't complain about a thing. They have all been very good to me. I have a neighbor across the street—Ethel Estlow—who brings me food all the time. She loves to cook, and I love to eat, so it's a good combination."

As I bade Marilyn and Pumpkin farewell, I realized that, like Alice, I have seen a cat without a grin, but at Buzby's Chatsworth General Store, I never saw a grin without a cat.

Endnotes

1. John McPhee, *The Pine Barrens* (New York: Farrar, Strauss and Giroux, 1967), 78–79.
2. R. Marilyn Schmidt, National Register of Historic Places Registration Form (NPS Form 10–900a), April 21, 2004.
3. Henry Charlton Beck, *Forgotten Towns of Southern New Jersey* (New Brunswick, NJ: Rutgers University Press, 1936), 99.
4. Schmidt, National Register of Historic Places Registration Form.
5. Everett Applegate, *Escape From the Pines* (Cassville, NJ: Cloonfad Press, 2006), 165–166.
6. Schmidt, National Register of Historic Places Registration Form.
7. Jason Method, "Wiener Wars," *Burlington County Times*, August 1, 1989, A1.
8. Jason Method, "Father-Daughter Team Continues Hot Dog Sales," *Burlington County Times*, August 13, 1989, A1.
9. Jason Method, "The Buns Are Back in Town," *Burlington County Times*, August 13, 1989, A1.

From Cranberries to Christ

It was late afternoon when I turned down the driveway of Camp Haluwasa in Hammonton. I had been driving for an hour and a half in the Pine Barrens and was starting to spike a fever from a sinus infection I had been fighting. I guess I must have looked a little battle worn as I pulled in because the 88-year-old Reverend Charlie Ashmen offered to drive *me* around the place. I felt a twinge of guilt as I gratefully climbed into his passenger seat.

Charlie explained that he had just been given the car by a woman for whose family he had performed a number of funeral services. She had remarked to him that pastors in the area seemed to come and go so quickly that you didn't get a chance to know them. He told her he had been there for 52 years, and apparently this longevity impressed her because soon afterward she donated the vehicle.

As I drove around with Charlie that afternoon, I learned that most of what he had on the property had either been donated or bought at bargain prices.

Charlie and I started out at the southern end of the property, driving across an embankment that held a lake to the right and railroad tracks to the left. It was late October—Indian summer—and a few cold nights had coaxed brilliant colors from the maples reflected by the lake's surface.

The placid waters of the lake stretch 800 feet across; the far end opens into a second lake, and beyond that, into a third. All together, these lakes are nearly a mile long, with about 2 miles of shoreline. The lakes are called *HeKeMeSi*, *MoLiThMa*, and *MyAnHo*—names that are actually taken from the first few letters of the title words of Charlie's favorite hymns: "He Keeps Me Singing," "More Like the Master," and "My Anchor Holds."

On lazy summer days, sailboats and canoes traverse the quiet surface. Beneath the occasional ripples, bass, sunfish, and pickerel play. Gentle gusts brush along the sandy shores, causing fallen leaves to dance and swirl in random patterns.

The breeze cooled my fevered face, and I felt myself relaxing as I surveyed the peaceful scene. "We built those lakes, you know," Charlie said, snapping me out of my daydream.

"Excuse me?" I asked, convinced that my fever had gotten the best of me. "Did you say you *built* the lakes?"

"Yup," Charlie replied matter-of-factly, as if he had just told me he had built a sandcastle on the beach. "We bought this land for taxes; it was just swamp—old abandoned cranberry bogs."

I listened in rapt attention as Charlie began to tell me how Camp Haluwasa was born. The story begins in the 1950s, more than 1,500 miles from these woods, in the Colorado Rockies in a Christian camp called *Id-Ra-He-Je*, short for the hymn title "I'd Rather Have Jesus." Charlie, who had recently been a seminary student, and his wife, Nellie, got involved in ministry at the camp when they headed west on their honeymoon. They stayed on at the camp, and on one of their trips back home to New Jersey, they were inspired to start a similar camp here.

In 1954, America had 60,000 churches that were closed, and 15,000 villages without a Sunday school.[1] Charlie's dream was to provide a camp like the one he and Nellie had left in the Rockies—a place where young seminary students could serve rural areas.

The dream seemed to be a stretch at best for the young man only a few years out of seminary and with a wife and baby to care for. A pastor in Winslow Township jokingly told Charlie that there was some swamp land available in Hammonton for a good price.

Almost 3 decades earlier, the former owners had tried to cultivate cranberries on the parcel; their failed efforts left the land lush but badly overgrown. Despite the acres of dense brambles, Charlie saw potential in the stream that drew 100,000 gallons of water per hour from the ground. And the asking price was attractive: $2,000 for 114 acres.

The township was anxious to remove the land from the unpaid-tax rolls, but word of some "outside interest" in it traveled quickly. The township decided to auction the land instead, and on the day of the public auction, there was standing room only in the tiny town hall. Charlie brought his friend Frank along to bid for him. Frank squeezed into the last seat; Charlie stood in the doorway.

Charlie and his supporters waiting in the hallway had assembled $400 for the purchase. They were not aware that the winning bidder was required to secure his bid with 10 percent down in cash. The bidding quickly passed the $2,000 mark. Frank, aware of the deposit requirement, faithfully made his pitch for the property: $3,000 ... $3,200 ... $3,500. Once the bidding passed $4,000, though, he fell silent.

The bidding continued: $5,000 ... $6,000 ... $6,500 ... $6,800. Charlie watched his property slipping away as Frank said nothing. Finally Charlie moved up and poked Frank hard in the ribs, so Frank mumbled "$7,000." There was silence. No one countered the offer; $7,000 once, $7,000 twice. The auctioneer began lauding the land billed as a dismal swamp by the township only a few weeks earlier. He told the crowd that the stream pumped 100,000 gallons an hour, that there were 16 kinds of trees, and so on. At last, with no further response, he banged his gavel and brought the bidding to a close.

Charlie was elated—the property was his! He went outside to celebrate and found Frank pacing in circles. "What's the matter? We won the bid," Charlie said gleefully. Frank explained that the 10 percent deposit had to be paid within the hour or they would lose the bid. Charlie decided to pray. Just then, two ladies exited the building. One woman said, "How did you make out, Charlie?"

"Well," he said, "we won the bid, but we don't have enough to secure it."

The woman asked Charlie how much more he needed, and he said, "$300."

"Well, today's Friday and I just got paid," she said, reaching into her purse and handing Charlie her pay. Her companion followed suit, and suddenly Charlie had the $700 he needed. When they made the deposit, the township attorney warned them that they would lose the land if they didn't come up with the remaining $6,300 within 30 days.

So they prayed again that weekend. On Monday, a fellow who used to play saxophone with Charlie in Colorado called and asked what Charlie was doing these days. Charlie described his dream for a camp in the New Jersey woods. The fellow said he liked what Charlie and Nellie had done with Id-Ra-He-Je and offered a loan of $1,000, interest free, saying Charlie could pay it back whenever he was able. Another man, overhearing the phone conversation, made the same offer. Over the next 26 days, the money rained in, and by the end of the month, the Ashmens had the $6,300 they needed to achieve their dream.

Charlie's father was a machinist, so Charlie had grown up around motors and other moving parts. During World War II, Charlie worked as a marine machinist, building turbines and putting engines into warships. His love of machinery literally paved the way for Camp Haluwasa; he couldn't afford the $16-per-hour fee to rent a bulldozer, but he was offered free use of one if he could get it running.

Before long, trees were felled, and the dense underbrush gave way to trails through the marshland. The property was rich in sand and gravel, which was used to build the roads and later the rail beds for Haluwasa's unique train system.

An array of donated and low-cost vehicles joined the fleet, much like the car Charlie was ferrying me around in the day we met. As we drove over the dam between the two lakes, a water park came into view. Zip lines crossed part of the lake, and a dock waited silently for the kids to return next summer.

A 60-foot plastic water slide rises from the lake bank. Charlie explained that the slide had been donated and told me that after the people at the camp had put it up, they found that all sorts of permits and insurance were required if it was more than 5 feet off the ground. Charlie laughed nostalgically as he pointed to the hill surrounding the slide. "We got the bulldozer and created a hill under the slide," he said, his blue eyes twinkling, "and as you can see, the slide is never more than 5 feet off the ground anywhere."

Many of us have heard that God can move mountains, and in South Jersey, it seems He uses mechanics such as Charlie Ashmen to accomplish such tasks. But how do you build lakes?

Well, in the late 1950s, the cost to dig a bed around a stream and dam it up was about $20,000. Enter Charlie's ingenuity. Because the land used to contain cranberry bogs, Charlie "went up to Chatsworth to see how they fill up their bogs." What he found was that wooden flood gates are used to control the water level. He studied the design, salvaged wood from an old barn on the property, and soon had three lakes that he figures cost him about $15 in nails and spare parts.

Charlie's wry sense of humor is contagious, and his speech is punctuated with thought-provoking remarks, such as "If you were accused of being a Christian, would there be enough evidence to convict you?" "The trouble in the garden was not the apple on the tree, but the pair on the ground," and "Keep your words soft and sweet—you may have to eat them." His secret of running a coed camp? "We put the girl campers on one side of the lake and the boys on the other side; this way, we don't need to teach swimming!"

As a Christian camp, Haluwasa stages biblical plays each week. One week, David defeats Goliath with his slingshot, and the next, Elijah defeats the prophets of Baal. "We came up with a way to rig up the lake so it can part like the Red Sea," Charlie said, "but what's held us back is that we haven't figured out where to get new Egyptians each summer."

The reference to Egypt prompted Charlie to ask about me about New Egypt, where I live. I was impressed that he had remembered this from a passing comment and complimented him on his good memory.

"I can hear well too," he said. I was taken aback, thinking he must have assumed my comment was age-related, but before I could explain myself, he said, "I used to be a road captain in a motorcycle club; the boys who didn't listen got killed." I wasn't sure what to make of the sobering remark. I assumed he was just kidding around somehow.

I later read the story of this gutsy, unconventional preacher in *The Apples in a Seed: Haluwasa's Story of Vision.* Author Lloyd Mattson shared this vignette:

> A fun-loving motorcyclist approached a large tent not far
> from the Colorado River one evening. A sign reported

that an Eastern preacher was holding evangelistic meetings. The cyclist considered that a challenge. He revved up his machine and roared down on the tent, yelling as he sped past, "Glory, Hallelujah!"

The next day, the young cyclist spotted a small group near the tent chatting with a man he took to be the preacher. He drifted close. "Hey, Preach, let me give you a ride!"

The youthful minister smiled apprehensively at the cyclist. "I don't know if I'd care to ride a machine like that," he said. Then, as a hesitant afterthought, "Tell me how it works. Maybe I'll try it."

The cyclist grinned gleefully, explaining the controls of the huge cycle. To the dismay of the tent congregation, the preacher straddled the machine, fumbled the engine to life, and wobbled down the dirt road. Cycle and rider disappeared from view, weaving from side to side.

Suddenly there was a roar, the cycle headed toward the group, its engine snorting, dust flying. "How do you stop this thing?" screamed the preacher as he tore past. A turn in the road carried him from view. The men raced for their cars to retrieve the body of their minister.

But before they could drive off, the cycle returned to view, bearing down on the terrified cycle owner. Cutting a crisp figure-eight, the cycle reared like a bucking bronc and swerved to a halt at the owner's feet. "You better take this thing away, son. It looks dangerous to me," said the preacher.

The young cyclist had just met Charlie Ashmen, who had traded in his cyclist's leathers and road captain insignia for a Bible. Charlie had ridden with the Hell Cats, an Eastern contemporary of the Hell's Angels. A

rider who could fix bikes was invaluable, and other quali-
ties emerged that soon earned Charlie the title of road
captain.[a]

It was hard for me to imagine this gentlemanly, octogenarian
preacher as a motorcycle-riding spitfire. But I was still learning about
Charlie's true spirit. I asked him about the neck brace he was wearing, and I wasn't prepared for that answer either.

Charlie said that while one of the men was coupling trains in the
camp's railroad station, one car hit another, and the force sent four
loose cars careening down the track. From farther down the track,
Charlie saw the unmanned cars hurtling toward the bridge and some
campers who were fishing from it. He recognized the danger immediately. "They were standing on the track to fish, and there was no
place for them to go," he said. "They would have been killed."

Eighty-eight-year-old Charlie raced to cut off the wayward cars,
reaching the lead car just in time to block the rail ahead of it. The
momentum caught up with him, and he spilled over the ties. When
he got up, blood and cinder were smeared across his forehead.

"They wanted to take me to the hospital, but I told them I was
fine," Charlie recalled. "Nellie patched me up—she's good at that. A
few days later, I woke up, and my neck was all stiff and I couldn't turn
my head, so I went to the doctor, and they gave me an MRI. I cracked
a few of the vertebrae in my neck, so they're making me wear this
thing for a few weeks. But as long as the kids were all right."

I was still absorbing this story as we arrived at the cafeteria: an
imposing building nearly 200 feet long with wood-beam vaulted
ceilings and a baby grand piano for services and entertainment. "Do
you play?" he asked. I shook my head as he tapped a few keys harshly.
"Maybe someday I'll learn," he said wistfully as the painful sounds
continued.

I turned away from the old piano's groaning and hadn't even taken a step when the instrument burst into a vibrant, fast-paced patriotic song. The first chorus melded into another quick tune, and then Charlie rounded it off with a gospel hymn.

He had me with the first note. I found out later that he was self-taught, having learned to play by watching and copying the action of a player piano.

As he closed the cover on the baby grand, Charlie explained that as the camp grew, it needed a larger place for meals and meetings, but he had only $300 to cover the cost.

"There was a military establishment, and I found out that they had an old building they were going to sell," Charlie explained. "It was big enough to make a dining hall, so I asked them about it. They said there was nothing there but the frame, but we could have it for $1,400. So I told them that we didn't have that kind of money, so we'd wait a while and maybe it would be cheaper, and I began to pray about it.

"He called again and said 'I got your price—$1,300.' I said, 'I'll wait longer.' He called about a week later and said, 'You still want that building, Charlie?' I said I couldn't afford it, and he said, 'maybe you can now—an army truck backed up and knocked a big hole into it.' I came up and looked at it, and sure enough, there was a hole right where we wanted to cut out for our fireplace, so I said, 'We'll take it.'"

As I admired the beautiful stone and mortar fireplace—also made possible by local donations—it was hard to believe it hadn't been planned this way.

Haluwasa's pride and joy is its 24-gauge railroad, lovingly built by Charlie and his dedicated crew. It is the country's longest railroad of its kind, with 3 miles of track through the Pines. According to Charlie, the train serves a very practical purpose: "When parents bring their kids to camp, they're all teary eyed, and the mothers are standing around pretending to help the kids unpack but not wanting to leave, which makes it harder for the kids to settle in." With a train, he explained, the kids hop in with all their stuff, the whistle blows, and the parents are left at the station to wave goodbye.

The $12,000 price tag for the train's steam engine made this particular part of the Haluwasa dream a bit of a long shot, but one day Charlie came across a photo of a diesel engine that he thought might work. He bought some parts and built the locomotive from the photograph, using a Chrysler fluid drive that eliminated the need to shift gears. Charlie's ventures to local junkyards yielded the rest of the train's needs: an air-pressurized windshield wiper motor powers the bell, and Rambler differentials run the wheels. The cars were being advertised in catalogs for $1,200 each, but Charlie's crew was able to build them for about $60 apiece. The tracks run through the oversized garage, where an amazing assortment of drills, saws, and other tools is kept. This setup allows the crew to regularly inspect, maintain, and repair the train, even in the middle of the winter.

Nothing goes to waste at Camp Haluwasa. When new camping regulations rendered the original bunkhouses obsolete, they were moved to an island in the lake and resurrected as Frontier Village. Old water tanks were sliced open and welded together to make a bridge to the island.

Camp Haluwasa served the needs of 1,700 campers in 2008. Through the successful Angel Tree program, children with one or both parents in jail can attend camp through a scholarship program funded by generous donors. The kids come from all walks of life and all parts of the region. Charlie believes that if you feed the needs of children physically, mentally, and emotionally, you lay the groundwork for them to be fed spiritually as well. He said that many children have come to accept Christ at the camp, and campers often return in later years with friends and family members in tow.

And what does the name *Haluwasa* represent? Well, on dedicating this land once used to grow cranberries as a place to be used for Christ, Charlie could only say, "Hallelujah, What a Savior!"

Endnotes

1. Lloyd Mattson, *The Apples in a Seed: Haluwasa's Story of Vision* (Duluth, MN: Camping Guideposts, 1983), 19.
2. Ibid., 13–15.

Fire and Rain

There's something about a train that brings out the child in all of us. Charlie Ashmen knows this well; it's why he built the country's longest 24-gauge railroad—all 3 miles of it—on the grounds of Haluwasa, his Christian camp in Hammonton.

The thought of trains running through the Pine Barrens may seem strange to some people, but in the years following the Civil War, trains were an important means of transportation in South Jersey. While R. Marilyn Schmidt was preparing applications to have Buzby's General Store placed on the state and national historic registers, she compiled the following information regarding trains in the Chatsworth area, beginning after the Civil War:

> After the war, the main emphasis in the Pine Barrens was on fruit culture. Peaches and grapes proved profitable in Hammonton, Egg Harbor City, and Vineland, but attempts to grow peaches in this area ultimately proved a disaster. However, the Pine Barrens bogs proved ideal for

the cultivation of cranberries, which also grew in the wild. In the mid 1840s, artificial bogs were created [in Chatsworth].

In 1866, prices soared as a cranberry craze swept the northeastern markets. The price of land in the Pine Barrens increased accordingly. By the mid 1870s New Jersey was producing over half of the nation's cranberries. From the late 1860s to the early 1900s, a large share of this crop was sent to market over the railroads. During this period, Shamong Station prospered because of its association with this trade.

The panic of 1873–79 hit the marginal Pine Barrens industries hard. The factories in nearby Pasadena closed. The depression greatly interfered with the railroad's plans for expansion and reorganization. Unemployment increased and some residents were forced again to live off the land.

However, in the late 1870s, the railroad received an unexpected boost. Previous solutions to developing the Pine Barrens had not been successful. In the late 1870s the Lakewood hotel boom began.

The years 1887 to 1893 marked the period of the most extensive real estate promotions in the Pine Barrens. All were unsuccessful. The most notorious Pine Barrens development of this period was at Paisley, a village between Chatsworth and Tabernacle, and about 2.5 miles from Harris Station. Fourteen hundred acres were advertised as the "Magic City." Over 3,100 lots were sold, but the settlement contained only a dozen houses and a ramshackle one-story factory along unpaved roads. Nonetheless, all of these activities brought people to Chatsworth, primarily by train.[1]

Bob Lees, of Tabernacle, said, "I remember when everything in this area, for the most part, came by railroad. There was a railroad station in Smithville, there was one in Mt. Holly, there was one in Medford, and there was even a narrow gauge railroad in Vincentown; the others were the standard gauge. Milk was hauled out of Mt. Holly and out of Medford; a lot of the dairy farmers around here took their milk to Medford. First it went by wagon and then by railroad car; we didn't have milk trucks around here until the late '30s or early '40s. That was the most important thing when we had bad weather around here. We didn't worry about getting the public on the highways; we worried about getting the milk trucks in 'cause you could only hold milk for so long. First we worried about the milk, then we worried about getting the roads cleared, and lastly about getting the school kids in. If you had a major snowstorm, you didn't go to school unless you were close enough to walk."

Many longtime Pine Barrens residents have memories of walking along the tracks and of catching a train to school or to a job in Philadelphia or New York. Dina Napoli grew up in the Lanoka Harbor area. "As children, we used to go up to the railroad tracks," she told me. "We were told that there was a ghost—that he was an engineer, and he had died, and he couldn't leave the railroad tracks—so we were afraid to go there at night. I don't know how true it was—it might have been something our parents told us to keep us away.

"We used to go running down there and put a penny on the track before the train came so we would get a flat penny. But the really big thrill was who had the nerve to walk across the trestle when the train was coming." The trestle Dina refers to is on the Cedar Creek Campground property in neighboring Bayville. It stands about 12 feet above the sandy bottom of Cedar Creek and is in a sad state of decay.

"It was just the ties and the rail, and you had to step right or you could fall through," Dina explained. "You could put your ear to the rail and listen to tell if the train was coming. You couldn't jump off because it was too shallow and you would get hurt." Dina never attempted the crossing, but she knew many boys who did.

One boy jumped off for unknown reasons and died, according to one worker at Cedar Creek. "Because of the current, it took a week before they found his body," she said. "There was a story being passed among the canoeists, during that week that he was missing, to be careful or a hand might reach out and grab you."

One woman told me that, when she was in the fifth grade, she and her friends put pennies on the track while waiting for the train after school. "Then the boys told us that by doing that, we would make the train fall off the track. We had only wanted to flatten them. But we believed the boys. Me and my girlfriends started crying, saying 'We shouldn't have done that,' and we were so scared and upset. Of course, it was fine, and after that we did it all the time. We would pick the pennies up after the train crossed, and they would be so flat and hot."

Mahala Landrum, of Forked River, recalled that around 1920, the high school students would take the train into Toms River. She told us the train pulled in just around the time that classes were starting, and the students made so much noise trekking in that the principal told them they weren't allowed to come by train any more. So the school district had to hire a bus.

As buses and cars became more prevalent, the need for train service died out, but not before one of the most famous trains in the country made its way through the Pines.

"The Pine Barrens came alive with the Blue Comet," according to Charlie, who recalled that the famous train line passed right by Haluwasa. "It's why we built the railroad at the camp—kids love trains."

The Blue Comet was unique. Billed as the Seashore's Finest Train, it took passengers from New York City to Atlantic City in 3 hours. The cars were painted Packard Blue for the sky, Royal Blue for the sea, and along their sides, Jersey Cream for the sandy beaches. Joe Spooner, secretary-treasurer-editor of *Railroad Evangelist Magazine*, described the Blue Comet this way:

> The locomotives were painted a combination of royal and Packard blue with gold striping and lettering and nickel-plated cylinder heads along with other fittings. The coach cars had blue carpet in the aisles with leather seats and blue and white tile floor. The observation cars were furnished with two rows of twenty-four silver blue reed armchairs upholstered in blue plush, and blue carpets with a comet design worked in gold. The dining car had old frosted arched windows that had been painted over, but were visible from the inside dining area. The glass was replaced by an etched design of a comet, stars, and clouds. The table lights had parchment shades painted with gold stars and comets, while the deck lights had blue bulbs for subdued lighting. Special timetables, tickets, and baggage checks, printed on blue stock, were issued. Each train carried a porter outfitted in a French-blue uniform with French-blue vests and striped trousers.[2]

The Blue Comet had three new G3 Pacific locomotives. "The whistle came from a steamboat on the Mississippi River," Charlie told me. "You could hear the whistle blow from 9 miles away. I spoke to a guy on the station one very cold morning, and he said they blew the whistle, but he never heard it because the steam went up and froze."

Charlie described a dining car menu from its early days. "You could get a roast beef dinner with dessert for $1.23." The train line offered a Blue Plate Special, of course, for only 75 cents. The dining car was a source of pride, with its inlaid wood interior and tables graced with fine linens and silver. The Blue Comet logo even appeared on the menus.

The Blue Comet, pride of Central New Jersey's fleet, came to life on February 21, 1929. Each train consisted of 16 cars, named for comets. The diner was called Gicobini; the two combine-smokers, Halley and Encke; the baggage cars, Olbers and Barnardi; the eight coaches, Tuttle, Holmes, Westphal, D'Arrest, Faye, Spitaler, Winnecke, and Brorsen; and the three observation cars, DeVico, Biela, and Tempel.[3]

The train made two round-trips daily from its inception, with extra trips on Fridays and weekends during the summer. Stops included New York City, Jersey City, Elizabethport, Red Bank, Lakewood, Lakehurst, Hammonton, and Atlantic City. Along the way, the crew members would often toss their newspapers out for the people of the Pines to read.[4] Some of the folks I spoke with remember going to certain spots to get the paper. It is said that people brought berries and other treats to the Lakewood station for the crew.

The Blue Comet ran on schedule 97 percent of the time. Several highway overpasses along the train's route posted its schedule, and people would often stop and watch as it blazed down the rails.

On August 19, 1939, however, the Blue Comet missed its schedule. Heavy rains and strong winds moved into the northeast region that morning. The U.S. Weather Bureau at Trenton reported that 14.81 inches of rain fell on Tuckerton that day. Bureau chief A. E. White stated, "The amount of rainfall was phenomenal, and I believe it was the heaviest recorded in the history of the New Jersey bureau."[5]

The *Burlington County Times-Advertiser* reported the following in its August 23, 1939, issue:

> A record one-day rainfall occurred here Saturday morning wreaking havoc with farmers' crops and flooding sections along the banks of the Rancocas Creek.

The Chatsworth Cranberry Company reported the heaviest rainfall for this section with a measurement of 13.5 inches, while Lebanon Forest was next with 9.29 inches. Whitesbog measured 8.5 inches, Camp Remount CCC, Wrightstown, 6.7 inches and the Pemberton Experimental Station 5.71 inches. Officials in the Forest Experimental Station reported that 8.14 of the total 9.29 inches fell within a six hour period between 10 am and 4 pm. A 15-inch gauge at the Sterling Otis bogs, Tuckerton, overflowed, so heavy was the rain there.

More than 400 soldiers and CCC workers from Fort Dix worked all Sunday night to prevent the swollen Rancocas from halting operations at the Dix water pumping station at New Lisbon. Every available man in the garrison was summoned to the scene at 3 pm Sunday to construct a temporary dam of sand-bags.[6]

Other papers noted that 23 bridges on state and county highways were washed out and that dams in Chatsworth and New Lisbon burst. The driving rains washed out the roadbed at a culvert 3 miles south of Chatsworth. The tracks dropped several inches but did not break free from the ties.

The Blue Comet was ordered to proceed at half speed because of the weather. The *New York Times* would later report on its fate as it approached Chatsworth:

> The locomotive passed over the weakened tracks at the culvert without mishap, but the tender jerked, broke the coupling and jumped the rails, pulling five observation cars after it as it jounced over the ties.
>
> Tearing up and splintering the ties but not pulling up the tracks, the train came to a grinding stop when the first three cars careened against the embankment on the left

side of the train, the fourth car leaning precariously on a small embankment on the right side next to a stream, and the fifth, the diner, sloped the opposite way.

Passengers screamed as they feared the cars, all at steep angles, would overturn, but none did so. Of the forty-nine passengers, most of those who were injured were in the last two cars.[7]

Amazingly, only three people were seriously injured; one of them—a chef—was badly burned when an oil stove caused a small fire. He was dragged to safety by the train's crew. The remote location of the crash posed a challenge in getting first aid to the area, as the story in the *Times* documented:

Ambulances were summoned from towns throughout South Jersey and state troopers from barracks at Hammonton, Bordentown and Columbus. Since the accident occurred in the heart of the Central Jersey pine belt, just south of the Lebanon State Forest and about thirty miles north of Hammonton, it was several hours before aid could reach the vicinity after the accident was reported by a fireman who walked to a telephone.

Then the three seriously injured and about a dozen other passengers who were unable to walk the ties were brought on stretchers on a hand-car to Chatsworth, which was as near as the ambulances could come, the only dirt road having been washed out.

A relief train carrying passengers of the Blue Comet Express from the scene of the wreck near Chatsworth, NJ arrived at the Jersey Central Terminal here at 1:39 this morning. ... Among the passengers was Mrs. Margaret Sciria with her two year-old-daughter, Lillian. Mrs. Sciria told of carrying her child in her arms two and a half miles along the railroad tracks, walking the ties, sometimes wading in water up to her hips, to reach the relief train.

"The baby looked on it as a lark and laughed the whole time in spite of the rain, but I didn't feel like laughing as I trudged along," she said. Neither was injured.[8]

Falling ridership due to the Depression, competition from other lines, and improved road transportation led to the demise of the Blue Comet on September 27, 1941.[9] Locals may tell you, on certain rainy summer nights, that the lonesome whistle of that old line can still be heard in the wind.[10]

***

One of the Pennsylvania Railroad lines that ran from 1864 until 1977 ended at the Pemberton station,[11] out of which both of Lois Ward's grandfathers worked—one as an engineer, the other as a conductor. Speaking of her grandfather the engineer, Lois said, "If I had been good all day, when my grandfather came home from working, he would let me sit up in the chair and ring the bell before he put the train to sleep. I was about 4 years old at the time, and I've always loved trains. It was sad when they closed the station."

There was a spur at that station for the train to run up to the Pemberton Lumber and Millwork plant across the tracks. The plant produced prefabricated houses and buildings for U.S. and overseas customers and was one of the township's largest employers in 1945. On Friday, April 11, something went terribly wrong, and the building exploded in flames.

The *Burlington County Times-Advertiser* reported the disaster:

Origin of the fire is not known. It started at 1 PM in a corner near the front of the building in the dipping room where flooring is treated with an inflammable liquid.

Oliver McDowell, an employee, working outside, discovered flames pouring from the side of the building and notified the office force, which turned in the alarm.

A few moments after the blaze was discovered, drums of the preservative exploded, rattling house windows blocks away. Drums of the inflammable liquid continued to explode throughout the holocaust. Some barrels were hurled one hundred feet into the air.

Pemberton volunteer firemen laid hose 150 yards to a fire plug, but by the time they had water on the blaze the flames had spread to a railroad loading platform one hundred feet away. Within one hour the entire plant, covering an area 460 feet long and 200 feet wide, was completely enveloped by the flames. Firemen from twelve neighboring towns were unable to cope with the huge fire and concentrated on saving smaller buildings and piles of lumber threatened by the fire.

High winds fanned the blaze carrying sparks and burning embers across the Fort Dix-Pemberton Road.

Besides the plant and valuable machinery being destroyed, nine freight cars on a siding loaded with sections of pre-fabricated bungalows for France were destroyed. Another freight car, loaded with hardwood flooring within the plant, was gutted and nine other loaded freights on another siding were damaged by fire and would have been destroyed had not a locomotive rushed to the scene and pulled the cars to safety while firemen turned hoses on the flaming cars.[12]

The fire burned for days—by some accounts, for almost 2 weeks. Estimates of the damage to the mill ranged from $1 million to $3 million, and the Pennsylvania Railroad reported more than $300,000 in losses.

Lois lived across the street, and while her roof caught fire several times, the house did not burn down. "When the fire was bad, we would get out, but then we would go back in when they said it was safe," she recalled. "I remember taking the dogs out—we had two collies—and I would put them in the car. The firemen would come into the house and go up to the attic and make sure that there were no fires. I was about 12 years old. My dad said it burned for 2 weeks; they had fire companies from up north that came down to put it out. There was a gas station next door, and they were afraid that was going to blow."

Lois's husband, Earl, recalls, "When the wind blew, it scattered ashes all over town. I was a sophomore or junior in high school at the time, and they announced that the mill was on fire. We could see the smoke from our classrooms; we would sneak down and try to see it after school. We got as close as they would let us, but it wasn't very close. The mill had a couple of gas tanks next to the building to keep the trucks full, and they were burning. There was all this creosote, so it was hard to put out. Some of the train cars that came up to the building actually got welded right to the track because the fire was so hot."

The role of the railroad was an important one in the history of the Pine Barrens, allowing various industries to thrive as wares from the area were delivered to distant places such as New York and Philadelphia. Villages sprang up and grew in towns punctuated by railroad stops, and many old-timers fondly recall the sight of the Blue Comet whizzing through the Pines. As I travel south along Savoy Boulevard on my way to Chatsworth, I pass the old tracks of the Blue Comet and wonder what it must have been like to "watch it thunder by, a flashing blue comet on earthbound rails."[13]

Endnotes

1. R. Marilyn Schmidt, National Register of Historic Places Registration Form (NPS Form 10 900a), April 21, 2004.

2. Joe Spooner, "The Blue Comet: New Jersey Central," *Railroad Evangelist Magazine*, May–August 2005, 4–5.

3. Dorothy Voss, "The Blue Comet, 'The Seashore's Finest Train,'" *Telnews*, May 1986, www.geocities.com/Athens/Olympus/6745/Blue comet.htm (accessed January 5, 2009).

4. Ibid.

5. "Storm Damage Widespread in All Sections of the County," *New Jersey Mirror*, August 24, 1939, 1.

6. "Record Rain Floods Towns Along Rancocas," *Burlington County Times-Advertiser*, August 23, 1939, 1.

7. "Washout Derails Train, 17 Injured," *New York Times*, August 20, 1939, 1.

8. Ibid.

9. Spooner, "The Blue Comet: New Jersey Central," 4–5.

10. "The Blue Comet, Chatsworth, NJ 1939," Waymarking, March 2, 2008, www.waymarking.com/waymarks/WM39QT (accessed January 5, 2009).

11. Bill McBride, ed., "Hobo's Guide to the Pennsy: Pemberton and Hightstown Railroad," Keystone Crossing, kc.pennsyrr.com/Guide/Pemberton.Php (accessed January 5, 2009).

12. "3,000,000 Blaze Destroys P.L.&M. Plant," *Burlington County Times-Advertiser*, April 11, 1945, 1.

13. Spooner, "The Blue Comet: New Jersey Central," 4–5.

The Legend from Leeds

It was a chilly, starless night as I drove deep into the Pine Barrens. I had dressed in layers, as it was late October, and I didn't know how cold it might get after dark. The moon, nearly full, gave off an eerie glow through the clouds. The scraggly pines stood like sentries on either side of the road as I drove for 20 minutes without seeing another car. I watched in my rearview mirror as darkness enveloped the road behind me.

It was the perfect night to look for the Jersey Devil, and yet, I wondered why in the world was I doing this? Did I think there was any truth to the famous legend? And did I actually expect to encounter him here in these woods?

At least I had chosen a knowledgeable expert to lead me on this expedition. G. Russell Juelg, the director of outreach for the Pinelands Preservation Alliance, has been taking people on Jersey Devil hunts since 1997. An experienced woodsman, he is also the author of *New Jersey Pinelands: Threatened and Endangered Species*.

I asked Russell what got him interested in the Jersey Devil. He said he had read the book *The Jersey Devil*, by James McCloy and Ray Miller, and it had piqued his curiosity.

"I started going out in the Pine Barrens and looking for this thing," Russell said. "Of course, I didn't want to go by myself! So I always persuaded at least a few people to go with me. We'd go to a campsite, roast hot dogs and marshmallows, and then roam around in the woods to see if we might at least catch a glimpse of this bizarre creature.

"After a while, this guy called me and said he had heard about my Jersey Devil hunts. He said he used to think it was a bunch of silliness, but now he was changing his mind. He said he was an artist and could sketch animals. His neighbor came to him one day and wanted him to sketch an animal she had seen. He told her, if she could describe the thing, he could sketch it.

"He told me he kept working on the sketch until his neighbor was satisfied. 'Russell,' he said, 'if it wasn't the Jersey Devil, I don't know what it could have been. It looked sort of like a llama, with great big eyes and horns, standing on its hind feet. She said she saw it across the street from her house when she went out early in the morning to get her newspaper.'

"I have also heard stories from actual eyewitnesses," Russell continued. "A friend of mine told me she was out horseback riding with a few friends on a full-moon night. They went over this berm that separated a couple of old cranberry bogs, and suddenly her horse started to panic and try to veer to the right. She didn't see anything but a big mountain laurel shrub, so she kept coaxing her horse closer to it, to show her horse there was nothing to be afraid of.

"Her horse kept acting spooked, and finally she saw something behind the shrub. As she told me, 'At first I thought—oh, it's just a deer. But then I realized it couldn't be a deer, because it was standing upright, holding its front feet up. I kept trying to get a better look at it, but it kept slinking to the other side of the shrub, like it didn't want me to get too close. My horse was very frightened, so I finally rode away to catch up with my friends. We all rode back to the shrub to search for the creature, but we didn't find anything. This time my horse wasn't spooked at all.'"

Animals being spooked, crops failing, and milk turning sour have all been blamed on the appearance of the Jersey Devil. There are dozens of different accounts as to his origin and even more opinions about what he looks like and what trouble he has gotten into. Even his name has been debated: While most commonly referred to as the Jersey Devil (or "J. D." for short), he has also been called Hoodle-Doodle Bird, Wozzle Bug, and the Leeds Devil.

About the only thing the legend variations seem to agree on is that he was born in 1735 and that the name *Leeds* is somehow linked to him. According to the most popular version of the story, he was born to a woman named Leeds in the town of Leeds Point, New Jersey. She had 12 children already and had cursed the baby during childbirth, saying, "Let him be a devil!" On entering the world, the Leeds child sprouted wings and claws and flew up the chimney and out into the Pine Barrens, where he has lived ever since.

Another version gives the woman's surname as Shrouds but also locates her in Leeds Point. However, the devil's birthplace is variously identified as Bordentown, Burlington, Estelville (now known as Estell Manor), and Pleasantville. His mother has been described as a prostitute, a healer, a witch, a Quaker, and a young girl who emigrated from England to marry a man she never met (which would make her one of our earliest mail-order brides). His paternity has been called into question as well: A Daniel Leeds is commonly mentioned, but some tales credit Japhet Leeds—a minister, a Revolutionary War soldier, or the devil himself, depending on who you ask.

The story turns even more interesting when storytellers describe the Pine Barrens' most infamous native son. His head resembles that of a horse or collie, and he has cloven hoofs on his rear feet and claws on his front, a serpentine tail, and wings with a massive spread. Some liken him to a large bird and believe the myth is linked to sandhill cranes that once lived in the Pines; others describe his wings as batlike.

Because he is called a devil, religion often factors into the tales. Some feel that the mother entered into a pact with the devil, giving him the child in order to regain her youth; others believe that witchcraft links her to the underworld. One tale says she was cursed by a minister for refusing to denounce her Quaker roots. Many tales attribute the lack of devil sightings over a span of time to a minister who, through a certain rite, caused the creature to be held in bondage for 100 years.

Most of the stories combine various elements of other tales in a mix-and-match fashion, leaving a dizzying array of mathematical possibilities for how the devil got his start. One thing is certain, however: More than 1,000 people claimed to have heard or seen him during the week of January 16–23, 1909, including councilman E. P. Weeden of Trenton, who said he was awoken by the sound of flapping wings and discovered the prints of cloven hooves outside in the snow.

Newspapers from Pennsylvania to New York carried news of the sightings. The *Asbury Park Evening Press* offered this colorful account of one eyewitness:

> Millville, Jan. 22—Dan Possak of this place has had a terrific struggle with one of the strangest freaks of nature, or a monster straight from the bad place, that has ever been recorded. Dan was doing his chores when he heard someone walking through the backyard and calling to him. He turned and beheld a monster beast-bird about eighteen feet high.
>
> "Where do you keep the garbage can?" demanded the visitor, in as good English as Dan could use.

Too terrified to answer, Dan ran for the barn. Before he reached it the beast-bird caught him and wrapped its sinewy and scintillating red neck around his body. Dan happened to have a hatchet in his belt—he had been cutting kindling wood—and with this he commenced hacking at his assailant's body. He was astonished to find that he could chop splinters off of the body, just as tho it were of wood.

While he was chopping the beast-bird tightened the coils of its mile-end neck about his body and hissed something in his ear. With one last smash he crashed his hatchet into the head of the beast-bird.

Out dropped the eyeball, and with a scream of pain the assailant took in a long breath, filled its body like a balloon and floated up into space, leaving Dan and its right eyeball behind.

The eyeball looks like a new-fangled kind of electric lamp, and at night gives a blinding, dazzling light that turns different colors.[1]

There are many theories as to why the legend has persisted for almost 3 centuries. As with the "ghost engineer" tale told to Dina Napoli and her friends to keep them off the train tracks at night (see the chapter titled "Fire and Rain"), the Jersey Devil may endure as a means of keeping young people out of the Pines at night.

I shared these tales and the research I had done with Russell Juelg as he stoked the campfire. There were 13 of us scheduled to go on the walk that night, and we laughed over the irony of the number as we waited for the others to arrive. Russell had brought his banjo; he always opens with a few songs and invites those gathered to share any personal encounters they may have had.

I asked Russell to share one of the more unusual stories he has heard.

"Of course, sometimes people don't see the Jersey Devil; they just hear it," he said. "This happened to three young men I met one night. I was driving through the Pine Barrens on this little sugar sand road. It was quite dark. Up ahead I saw some light.

"When I got closer, I saw three guys standing around a big bonfire right in the middle of the road. They looked to be about the age of high school students, and they didn't appear to be dangerous, so I pulled up closer, and they walked over to the truck and greeted me.

"'Can you tell us where we are?' one of them asked. They explained that they had gotten their vehicle stuck in a deep muddy spot and that they had been walking for hours, trying to find their way out of the woods. I told them where they were and offered them a ride, and I asked them why they had built that fire in the middle of the road. After a moment of hesitation, they told me what had happened.

"'We kept walking, and finally it got dark. We started hearing a sound like an animal moving through the woods alongside us. We thought maybe it was a dog, so we called out to it, but it started making these high-pitched shrieking sounds. Then we thought maybe it was some kind of bird. We kept walking, but it kept following us, getting closer and closer. It started making these really loud howling sounds. We never heard anything like it. We decided to grab some dry leaves and sticks and make a big fire, hoping that would keep it away.'

"The young men and I were quiet for a moment, and we all glanced about at the dark trees. 'Did it leave after you made the fire?' I asked.

"'We never heard it leave,' they said, 'but it quit howling just about the time we saw your headlights in the distance.'

"'Well, guys,' I said, 'have you ever heard of the Jersey Devil?'

"'Yeah,' they said. 'But we thought that was just a story.'"

Endnote

1. "Claim They Have Seen Leeds Devil," *Asbury Park Evening Press*, January 22, 1909.

Superhero

The late morning sun streamed through the open blinds, casting harsh shadows on the white linoleum floor. A man in a green sweatshirt sat at the counter, sipping a cup of coffee as he thumbed through his newspaper. A black baseball cap sat on his head, white hair sticking out above the adjustable strap in the back.

White Formica-topped tables lined the wall. Two neatly tucked straight-back chairs with wooden rungs framed each table. A white-washed chair rail divided the oak paneling from the pumpkin-colored walls above. An American flag was mounted in the corner, next to the entrance.

"I put your picture away, sat down and cried today," belted out Kid Rock and Sheryl Crow from the radio behind the counter. "Since you been gone, my world's been dark and grey."

A waitress named Kim grabbed a dishtowel from behind the counter and began wiping down the table next to me. Her long, dirty blonde hair was swept up in a quick bun. She wore two shirts, one layered over the other.

"What can I get you to drink?" she asked, slapping a menu down in front of me. "Just water," I replied as I scanned the menu. My eyes fell on the weekly breakfast special: Piney omelet with 12 eggs, fresh possum, and Limburger cheese on a bed of pine needles for $12.50. With home fries, $14.75.

I was tempted to order it but opted for the pancakes instead. It was still early, and I hadn't worked up that much of an appetite yet.

More diners wandered in. Donna, another employee, came out of the kitchen and began busing the tables. The conversation was light and bantering. Kim teased the regulars as she refilled their coffee cups. Family pictures were tucked above the doorway to the kitchen. The walls held an eclectic collection of gifts donated by customers over the years: a numbered cranberry scoop, an illustration of the diner, a tree stump carved to look like the man in the moon.

Near the entrance was a framed collage featuring photographs of dozens of customers who have eaten here at Lucille's Country Cooking diner. Lucille Bates-Wickward, the diner's owner, considers many of these customers her friends.

"Some of the best friends I have today are people I met in here," Lucille said as she joined me at the table.

Besides doing the cooking, Lucille has another vital (some would argue even more important) role at the diner, that of social director. "People tell me that they don't come in here just for the food; they come in here for the conversation and atmosphere." This can include the occasional trivia question posed to customers.

What sets Lucille's Country Cooking apart from other diners in New Jersey is that complete strangers often strike up conversations with diners at nearby tables. More often than not, customers at all 10 tables will participate in a single conversation. Like well-rehearsed actors, they provide straight lines for the staff and participate in jokes played on unsuspecting employees.

"I am always saying: Don't try to be a superhero. If you need help, ask someone else to give you a hand. Don't try to do everything yourself," Lucille told me. "So one morning I came in, and we had four people working that day besides myself. I went into the kitchen, and the employees had tied large black garbage bags around their necks like capes. Usually I'm not fooled by their stunts, but when I saw them all wrapped up, I asked if they were cold.

"In sync, they all whirled around with their capes flying out behind them and shouted 'We're superheroes!' Before I could say anything, they marched out to the front in their capes. You should have seen the expressions on people's faces. Some were covering their mouths and trying to decide whether to laugh. So then I explained to everyone what they were doing, and the customers thought it was very funny. The employees really paid me back that day."

Sometimes the diners become the audience, eagerly awaiting the next act. "You know Kim and Donna are both blondes," Lucille deadpanned, setting the stage. The diners smiled in anticipation. "So yesterday we were at Wells Mills Park, catering the Pine Barrens Jamboree. Kim and Donna took separate trucks and each took a different road, ending up on opposite sides of the lake. Kim got out, walked to the water's edge, and yelled across to Donna: 'How do I get to the other side?' Donna got out of her truck, eyed the lake from one end to the other and replied, 'You *are* on the other side.'"

The diners roared with laughter—and immediately began trying to top one another with their own blonde jokes. Lucille has nothing against blondes; she has just learned firsthand not to take herself or life too seriously. This lesson did not come easy.

Thirty-two years ago, Lucille and her husband, Jim, purchased an empty building. Jim worked as a mechanic and planned to use it as a garage. It had been a turkey farm, but the sound of jet planes taking off from the nearby Warren Grove Bombing Range caused the turkeys to stampede and attack each other, according to Lucille.

"After we bought it, we found out that zoning permitted only four commercial uses for this site: a flower shop, a pet grooming shop, a beauty parlor, or food service, so we decided to make it a diner." Neither Lucille nor Jim had any prior food-handling experience or training.

"Now, at this point, I had been married to Jim for 15 years, and he was not able to put a sandwich with lunchmeat together—or so I thought. What I found out when we came in here was that he was an excellent cook. I was very nervous, and he would say, 'Just do what you do at home, only make bigger pots—make a bigger pot of soup, make a bigger pot of chili."

Lucille said she also learned how difficult it was to be in business with your mate—working side by side in the diner and then bringing it all home with them at night. They called their business the Warren Grove Snack Bar, but most of their customers referred to it as the Bates place.

After 4 years spent building up the snack bar and its clientele, Jim was diagnosed with cancer and died soon after. Their four children were ages 16, 12, 10, and 8. "I remember saying at the time," Lucille recalled, "I am only a woman and what can a woman alone do?" Scared and nervous about the future, she put the business up for sale.

"My friends and family kept reassuring me that I could do it," Lucille continued. She admitted to me that she got angry at God after Jim died. "I would just say, 'Why, God?' and then one day, a woman came to my house and told me that God would give me the strength to get through this. She was right. God doesn't prevent you from having heartache, but He gives you the strength to get through it."

Lucille took down the For Sale sign and got back to work. The children pitched in after school and during the summer. "This was the story of a family that really had to pull together," she said. "My children developed into better adults from really having to work from the time they came home from school. They peeled potatoes, made fresh hamburger meat patties, and mopped the floor. I have visions sometimes of my children when they were 8 and 10 years old, standing on a milk crate washing dishes at the sink."

Lucille's Country Cooking is surrounded by hunting clubs, and during the weeklong deer-hunting season in early December, the diner is always filled. "The first year," Lucille said, "I was here alone, and I couldn't do it, so I kept them all home from school. Naturally the school called and said, 'Where are your children?' and I told the school that they had to work. Even 25 years ago, that wasn't acceptable. I remember trying to explain to the school, 'They are learning math by using the register, they are learning to cook in the kitchen, and they are learning sociology dealing with people,' but the school didn't see it that way. So the next day, they all returned to classes."

Over the years, Lucille watched her children and the business flourish. "The customers were great to my kids. Sometimes customers would help with homework. One man would take the change out of his pocket and dump it on the table. He told my daughter that if she could count it correctly, it was all hers. If she got it wrong, he swept the coins back into his pocket for the next time.

"On days off from school or in the summer, my children had the opportunity to meet people from every walk of life. One day, they might be sitting next to a colonel from the air range and start talking to him; the next customer to walk in might be a local minister or priest, then a recycling garbage man. ... So they have been exposed to all sorts of people, all sorts of careers. I find they can get into a conversation with anyone."

Lucille's confidence grew along with that of her children. "I would have described myself as an introvert, but after many years of dealing with the public, as you can see, I've blossomed. I'm happy with the person I've turned out to be. I've been able to benefit from this. Looking back, I can't think of another thing I would rather have done in my life."

One of the things she is most proud of is her past work with domestic violence victims. She has also served as a member of the Stafford Historical Society, a Girl Scout leader, a Cub Scout leader, vice president of the Business and Professional Women of Southern Ocean County, and the only woman in the Lion's Club, among many volunteer roles. "I think back to 1980, when Jim died and I said 'I can't do this alone because I am just a woman.' Since then, I have been able to tell women, 'You can do far more than you think.'"

Lucille continues to learn from her customers and grow, and in many ways, she feels she has gained far more than she has contributed. She considers it a humbling experience.

"I think one of the hardest things in life is to lose a child," she told me solemnly. "I learned a long time ago not to say 'Happy Mother's Day' or 'Happy Father's Day' to people. The first time I said it in here to a customer, it was to someone who had lost a child, and the customer told me that it was not a happy time. Of course, I didn't know that when I said it, but I learned the lesson. Everyone—even if they seem happy or are laughing—has had some kind of problem in life."

Lucille says she has benefited from the advice of customers. An advertising executive once told her he would give her, free, what his clients paid him the big bucks for. His advice: Change the name of the diner. "Warren Grove Snack Bar," he said, "implied you could get a soda or candy bar, not breakfast and lunch."

"He told me to make the outside sign a red or yellow color and to use a person's name. He told me that people will remember the name of someone, but they won't remember the name of the town." She took his advice, and today *Lucille's Country Cooking* is emblazoned proudly in blue and red letters on a yellow sign facing Route 539.

***

Besides superhero capes, many costumes have made their debut in the diner. Lucille has come in wearing rainbow-colored clown wigs, red ball noses, and even a feather boa.

"A fellow came in here for lunch with his grandfather, who was living in a nursing home. He was probably in his late 80s and had Alzheimer's disease. I didn't know he had Alzheimer's. I came out with this feather boa, and I tickled his bald head with the feathers. He kinda laughed, and he ate his sandwich, and they left," Lucille recalled. "The other day, the young man came in here and told me that his grandfather has Alzheimer's and he can't remember anything. But he told his grandson that he wanted to go back to where the lady had the feathers—he remembered that part. The man was happy, and even his grandson laughed—they both got to smile that day, but I was happier than both of them."

Lucille's smile faded momentarily. "This is all lost now. Your waiter or waitress isn't usually joking around with you; there isn't a social butterfly limping around. I think if you find something nice to say to everybody and you are sincere, it really helps. Maybe it's the cologne they put on, the brooch they are wearing, or maybe a color that's good for them. Even if you say something small to people, it can brighten someone else's day."

Lucille serves a wide range of customers, from day-trippers exiting the Garden State Parkway for points north to southbound travelers gearing up to gamble in Atlantic City. In the morning, there are truckers; in the fall, hunters and fishermen; on Sundays, churchgoers. Lucille and her crew dish up hundreds of sandwiches to sustain the Forest Fire Service members and volunteer firefighters during the many blazes in the nearby woods. What's a firefighter's favorite sandwich? I flunked this trivia question.

"Peanut butter and jelly," she informed me. "If it's a big fire and they are going to be there a while, they tell me they can just shove the sandwich in their pocket until later and it will not spoil.

"I think our Forest Fire Service is the best in the whole country. When there is a forest fire, it is like an orchestrated event because they all work together, synchronizing their moves like a ballet being performed. The next thing you know, they have it all under control."

Lucille considers her business philosophy to be very basic. "I try to treat people the way I like to be treated. The food should be good and served hot or cold—whichever temperature it is supposed to be. It should be an ample quantity, of good quality, and priced right—the old-fashioned beliefs. Don't take advantage of your customers. That doesn't mean I need to have a conversation with every customer, but don't go skimping on the sandwich, because they are coming back tomorrow."

Lucille told me that she learns something new from her customers every day. "Something that has always amazed me are the people in their 80s who come in. They have been married for 50 or 60 years, and they still like each other. We just had a couple in here the other day—they are both 86 and have been married forever. They said they've had a couple of words between them over the years, but they still love each other and touch each other's hands across the table. This particular couple has traveled to every country in the world except China and India, and those are still on their agenda at 86!

"The older folks—if they will open up and get into conversation— have so much that they have experienced. I have been to many places in conversation that I will never personally get to visit. But I feel like I have been there when they get done telling me their experiences and the places they have seen, so I guess I go on a trip every day.

"I remember talking to a couple of men who were up in their 80s, and they had been rangers. They had stormed the beaches of Normandy, and they talked about their experiences. They opened up their wallets, and they had these little cards that were aged and worn; they had been in and out of their wallets many times. The cards said they were rangers. It was a very humbling moment to talk to someone who was there and survived."

Lucille said her only regret was not keeping a diary. "I have met at least one interesting person every day of my life. You think you are not going to forget these things, but you do, over time."

The diner started out serving three meals a day, 7 days a week, and Lucille worked from 5:00 AM to 9:00 PM. When her health began to fail in 1984, she had to reduce the hours to 7:00 AM to 3:00 PM. The effects of having been stricken with ovarian cancer, fibrosarcoma in her leg muscle, and renal cell cancer also forced her to curb her volunteer activities, but it didn't dampen her enthusiasm. "When I worked 14 hours, I was always running," she said. "Now I'm lucky that I'm able to walk."

Lucille may be walking with a slight limp these days, but she has made a remarkable recovery. Six weeks after her last cancer surgery, she was back joking with customers in the diner.

"I think I found my calling in life," she yells to Kim.

"What's that?" Kim responds.

"Being here," Lucille deadpans back.

Lucille attributes her quick recovery to the many prayers, cards, flowers, gifts, even home-cooked meals her customers sent her. "It would make you cry, the number of people who truly care about people. I was usually the strong one, but when I was on the bottom, people came out in droves.

"I have also learned that you have to surround yourself with happy people," she said. "Sometimes, when I start feeling a little self-pity, I see someone and realize that no matter how bad my experience has been, there is always someone worse off than I am. I am limping around, and then someone comes in with a wheelchair. There's always somebody who brings you back to the basics, and that's the opportunity you have when you're dealing with the public.

"I've had people walk in who look very healthy, and you start talking to them and find out they lost a breast to cancer. They had the strength to get through it, and I will, too. If I were retired and at home before I got sick, I probably wouldn't have recovered as quickly.

"I have really been the fortunate one to have been touched by so many people. Every day is a new experience, a new adventure. Not many people can say they go to their job happy ... and come home feeling rewarded, but I do every day.

"When it's my time to go, I will be leaving with a lot of happy memories. I live every day like it is my last. If you make somebody else happy every day, you'll be happy, too. Because the diner is small, we can really talk to people and do these things; they say, 'you made my day,' but they really made mine.

"I am glad I am here, I'm glad I walked this walk," Lucille said, smiling.

"I just called to say I want you ... come back home," Kid Rock and Sheryl Crow croon as the music winds down.

Epilogue

More than a few people will debate my choice of subjects for *Voices in the Pines* and wonder about some that were not included. I met many fascinating folks in the course of this project whose stories I did not use for one reason or another, and there were many more with whom I was not able to meet. Rather than try to be comprehensive, my goal was to represent a small slice of what life in the New Jersey Pinelands is all about. If I've invited debate, perhaps it means I have reached individuals who care passionately about the Pine Barrens. I hope you have enjoyed and have been entertained by these stories, that you will forgive any perceived oversights, and—most important, perhaps—that this book may inspire the merely curious to take a closer look.

The Pine Barrens has a rich and fascinating human history, but sadly we lose more of it every day. We need to listen to and preserve these stories now, while we still have those among us who are able and willing to share them.

I think of the women at Niki Giberson's Friday Friendship nights, who are learning basket making and the history behind the craft. These women are discovering something about themselves in the process, as well as leaving a legacy behind for future generations.

When tempers flared over the changing designs on the Painted Rock on Route 539, people weren't just racing down the road in a blur;

they were debating politics and patriotism and perhaps re-examining their own beliefs and attitudes.

When a hunter kills a deer, we either applaud the marksmanship, recognize the need to put food on the table, or react with revulsion or outrage over the act of taking the animal's life. In each case, we *feel*. We *think*. We must remember that all our actions impact society in some way. And that is the case with those folks living and working in the Pines. They are not as isolated a segment of society as we might like to think. They toil in the fields to harvest the blueberries and cranberries that we enjoy so much. They are our neighbors with singed faces and hands as they work to put out the next blaze that tears through the pines. They serve us food as we stop in their establishments on the way to Atlantic City, yet we barely give them a second thought as we head out and continue down the road.

While I have learned, over a period of many years, to love the Pine Barrens and to understand the region reasonably well from an environmental and historical viewpoint, the individuals interviewed for this book taught me what it means to have "a heart for the Pines." In almost every interview, ultimately one of us would raise the question, What is a Piney? There was a time when the term carried a distinctly negative connotation and was thus avoided. While there are still some who consider it derogatory, most people who call themselves Pineys today do so with a fierce pride. It's an honorable designation, and they've earned the right to use it.

Gary Giberson's family has lived in the Mullica River area of South Jersey since 1637. In addition to hunting, trapping, fishing, and making his living off the muck cedar trees that grow literally in his backyard, Gary has been mayor of Port Republic since 1984. Gary's diverse life experiences, rooted in the Pine Barrens, give him a unique perspective on the question, What is a Piney?

"A Piney is a neat person … a person who has a tie to the land and soil," he began. "A Piney doesn't have to be seven or eight or even nine generations, like myself. He can move here from another state, but he appreciates it and tries to protect it. He enjoys the beauty of canoeing in the Pines and learning about the animals. But he also must have respect for the people of the Pines."

I challenge outsiders to recognize how much there is to be learned from the Pineys and this wonderful land we call the Pine Barrens—and to gain this understanding before it's too late. Pola Galie, outreach coordinator for the Conserve Wildlife Foundation of New Jersey and caretaker of the Lighthouse Center in Waretown, said, "New Jersey is expected to be the first state in America to reach total build-out. When I first started working with the Conserve Wildlife Foundation, I found communication letters that said, 'Within the next 90 years, New Jersey may reach total build-out,' and 2 years later, they were saying 'within the next 30 years,' and that's really scary. We're the most densely populated state, and yet we're the northernmost area for some species and the southernmost area for others. We have so much diversity, so much more than other states have."

She continued, "It's places like the Pines that ultimately give us our quality of life. What would we do without the trees giving us air, without the ability to filter our water? All those things are so important, and we have to appreciate them. I don't want my grandson to have to go to a museum to see a tree. I want him to be able to make choices based on the resources we have. Considering that there is no other place on earth [like the Pine Barrens], I would want that to be his gift."

I think about Pola's and Gary's comments as I watch Andrew deftly putting the final touches on one of the illustrations for *Voices in the Pines*. I ponder the strange, twisting journey that Andrew and I have taken along these back roads, learning about industries and trades and people we didn't know existed when we started out.

How that respect for the Pineys has blossomed into a deep appreciation, reflected in the careful details that Andrew includes in his sketches, forever documenting lives that will soon disappear and return to dust. Since we embarked on this journey, Charlie Ashmen, Howard Steinmetz, and Cliff Oakley have passed on. They leave behind a legend that may one day be found only in books.

Some industries, such as cranberry production, will continue for years to come. But others, such as the charcoal industry, no longer exist in these woods. There will come a day when we will no longer be able to talk face-to-face with someone who picked pinecones from the pygmy pines to put food on the table or who gathered wild huckleberries to eat while traversing these woods. The one-room schoolhouses no longer house students, and sawmills no longer churn these waters.

The Pineys, with their unique way of life, are indeed a dying breed. So, too, is the open space in our state and country, as farms get plowed under to make way for the next development of homes or strip malls. As I watch Lucille lock up her diner after another full day and walk past the For Sale sign in her window, I think about how she taught me how she learns at least one new thing a day from the people who venture into her establishment.

If we take to heart the lessons and examples—the labor and efforts—of the Pineys who have gone before us, then maybe this is the legacy of the Pine Barrens that we can leave for generations to come.

References and Recommended Reading

Murder in the Pines

"Diner Operator Slays His Wife, Tries Suicide." *Asbury Park Evening Press*, March 31, 1953.

"Osmund Sand Succumbs to Bullet Wound." *Tuckerton Beacon*, April 9, 1953.

"Sand Succumbs; Shot Wife, Self." *Asbury Park Evening Press*, April 6, 1953.

"Tuckerton Wife Shot to Death; Husband Wounded." *Tuckerton Beacon*, April 2, 1953.

Stewards of the Land

Ocean Spray. "Cranberries May Reduce Inflammation Associated With Severe Gum Disease." *Ocean Spray*, July 10, 2006. www.oceanspray.com/news/pr/pressrelease103.aspx (accessed January 5, 2009).

Ocean Spray. "Cranberries Provide Urinary Tract Protection for Up to Two Years." *Ocean Spray*, August 13, 2007.

Ocean Spray. "Review Finds Cranberries Support a Healthy Heart." *Ocean Spray*, January 31, 2008. www.oceanspray.com/news/pr/

pressrelease118.aspx (accessed January 5, 2009). www.oceanspray.com/news/pr/pressrelease116. aspx (accessed January 5, 2009).

Age of Innocence

Applegate, Everett. *Escape From the Pines*. Cassville, NJ: Cloonfad Press, 2006.

Cervetto, Jack. *Living With the Pine Barrens*. Toms River, NJ: Ocean County Historical Society, 2000.

Battle at Painted Rock

Clunn, Nicholas. "Painted Boulder Provokes Man's Ire: Peace Signs Replaced Flag." *Asbury Park Press*, July 4, 2005.

————. "Rock Becomes Battleground for Passerby: Flag Repainted Over Peace Signs on Roadside Landmark." *Asbury Park Press*, July 17, 2005.

Heidorn, Keith C. "The Inferior Mirage: Not Just for Deserts Anymore." *Weather Doctor*, July 15, 1999. islandnet.com/~see/weather/elements/infmrge.htm (accessed December 28, 2007).

"Local Rock Artist Carves Out a Fanciful Niche on Route 539" [Letter to the Editor]. *Beach Haven Times*, January 24, 2001.

Ortiz, Susan. "New Jersey's Most Painted Rock." *WeirdNJ.com*, 2005. www.weirdnj.com/index.php?option=com_content&task=view&id=37&Itemid=28 (accessed January 14, 2009).

Palmer, Mary. "Topic of the Day: Roadside Artwork" [Letter to the Editor]. *Asbury Park Press*, July 15, 2005.

Rahn, Jim. "Rt 539 Painted Rock." jamesrahn.com, July 1, 2007. jamesrahn.com/personal/rock.htm (accessed December 29, 2007).

Shooting the Curl

Sadovi, Carlos. "Fire Burns 4,500 Acres." *Asbury Park Press*, June 14, 1992.

Section Forest Firewardens of Division B. *Images of America: New Jersey Forest Fire Service.* Charleston, SC: Arcadia Publishing, 2006.

"Wilderness Survival School Celebrates 25th Anniversary." *Tom Brown Jr.'s Tracker School,* December 10, 2003. trackerschool.com/news_press_details.asp?id=3 (accessed January 7, 2008).

Snared

Noonan, Bob. "Defying Death." *Trapper and Predator Caller,* January 2005: 22–26.

RADONS

Bates, Todd B., and Kirk Moore. "Federal Officials Draw Criticism Over Missile Site." *Asbury Park Press*, June 10, 1987, A8.

Beck, Eckardt C. "The Love Canal Tragedy." *USEPA Journal,* January 1979. epa.gov/history/topics/lovecanal/01.htm (accessed December 24, 2007).

Carroll, Cathy. "Judge Draws Crowd at the Site." *Ocean County Observer*, June 11, 1987, 1.

———. "Radon Vigil is Group's Labor of Love." *Ocean County Observer*, June 11, 1987, 3.

Chichioco, Marites, and Jo Ann Moslock. "Ocean Judge Blocks State From Moving Tainted Soil." *Asbury Park Press*, June 7, 1987, 1.

Christopher, Sam. "Judge Orders Dumping Stopped." *Ocean County Observer*, June 7, 1987.

Felzenberg, Alvin S. *Governor Tom Kean: From the New Jersey Statehouse to the 9-11 Commission.* Piscataway, NJ: Rutgers University Press, 2006.

Fröman, Nanny. "Marie and Pierre Curie and the Discovery of Polonium and Radium." *Nobelprize.org*, December 1,1996. nobel prize.org/nobel_prizes/ physics/articles/curie/index.html (accessed December 24, 2007).

Galant, Debbie. "Living With a Radium Nightmare." *New York Times*, September 29, 1996.

Grady, Denise. "A Glow in the Dark, and a Lesson in Scientific Peril." *New York Times*, October 6, 1998. query.nytimes.com/gst/ fullpage.html?sec=health&res=990DE1D61E38F935A35753C1 A96E958260 (accessed December 24, 2007).

Johnson, Tom. "DEP Acts to Store Radon Soil at Jersey Wildlife Preserve." *Star Ledger*, June 5, 1987.

Johnston, Jay. "Jackson Site to Get Radium-Tainted Dirt." *Asbury Park Press*, June 5, 1987, A1.

―――. "Radon Leaves Trail Through NJ Courts." *Asbury Park Press*, June 21, 1987, A3.

―――. "State Says Choice of Soil Site Was Not 'Arbitrary.'" *Asbury Park Press*, July 3, 1987, A1.

Kaye, Mel. "Radium Dial Painting and Its Tragic Consequences." *NAWCC Bulletin*, April 2005. nawcc.org/pub/articles/ apr05/apr05.htm (accessed December 24, 2007).

Mallow, Patricia A., and Roberta Wells. "Jackson, Plumsted Residents Mobilize." *Asbury Park Press*, June 9, 1987, A2.

―――. "Mayor Assured About Tainted Soil." *Asbury Park Press*, November 10, 1987.

McHugh, Bob. "Interior Head Opposes Radon Plan." *Ocean County Observer*, June 11, 1987, 1.

"Proposed Fed Trap Ban: Typical DC Bell Cow or Threat?" *International Foundation for the Conservation of Natural Resources Wildlife Ecology Website*, August 22, 2005. wildecology.ifcnr. com/article.cfm?NewsID=353 (accessed January 3, 2008).

Quinn, Susan. *Marie Curie: A Life*. Cambridge, MA: Da Capo Press, 1996.

Sullivan, Joseph F. "Rally Protests the Storage of Tainted Soils." *New York Times*, June 5, 1987.

"Superfund." *U.S. Environmental Protection Agency*. epa.gov/super fund/about.htm (accessed December 24, 2007).

Buzby's and The Cheshire Cat

Applegate, Everett. *Escape From the Pines*. Cassville, NJ: Cloonfad Press, 2006.

Beck, Henry Charlton. *More Forgotten Towns of Southern New Jersey*. New Brunswick, NJ: Rutgers University Press, 1937.

McPhee, John. *The Pine Barrens*. New York: Farrar, Strauss and Giroux, 1967.

Method, Jason. "The Buns Are Back in Town." *Burlington County Times*, August 13, 1989, A1.

———. "Father-Daughter Team Continues Hot Dog Sales." *Burlington County Times*, August 13, 1989, A1.

———. "Wiener Wars." *Burlington County Times*, August 1, 1989, A1.

"Some History of Lakehurst." *NY-NJ-CT Botany Online*. nynjct botany.org/njoptofc/lakehurs.html (accessed December 29, 2007).

From Cranberries to Christ

Ashmen, Charlie. *Charlie's Shop Talk: The Ministry of Machines and Maintenance*. Cotton, MN: Camping Guideposts, 1987.

Frame, Alan. "A Model Railroad in 2-Foot Gauge: The Haluwasa Shoreline Railroad." *Local/Mid-Eastern Region/NMRA*, January–February 2003, 14.

Mattson, Lloyd. *The Apples in a Seed*. Duluth, MN: Camping Guideposts, 1983.

Fire and Rain

"3,000,000 Blaze Destroys P.L.&M. Plant." *Burlington County Times-Advertiser*, April 11, 1945.

"The Blue Comet, Chatsworth, NJ 1939." *Waymarking*, March 2, 2008. www.waymarking.com/waymarks/WM39QT (accessed January 5, 2009).

McBride, Bill, ed. "Hobo's Guide to the Pennsy: Pemberton and Hightstown Railroad. *Keystone Crossing*. cc.pennsyrr.com/Guide/Pemberton.Php (accessed January 5, 2009).

Olsen, Judith Lamb. *Pemberton: An Historic Look at a Village on the Rancocas*. New Orleans: Polyanthos, 1976.

"Record Rain Floods Towns Along Rancocas."*Burlington County Times-Advertiser*, August 23, 1939.

Spooner, Joe. "The Blue Comet: New Jersey Central." *Railroad Evangelist Magazine*, May–August 2005.

"Storm Damage Widespread in All Sections of the County." *New Jersey Mirror*, August 24, 1939.

Voss, Dorothy. "The Blue Comet, 'The Seashore's Finest Train.'" *Telnews*, May 1986. www.geocities.com/Athens/Olympus/6745/Bluecomet.htm (accessed January 5, 2009).

"Washout Derails Train, 17 Injured." *New York Times*, August 20, 1939.

The Legend from Leeds

"Claim They Have Seen Leeds Devil." *Asbury Park Evening Press*, January 22, 1909.

"Near Million Dollar Fire Wipes Out Lumber Plant at Pemberton on Friday." *New Jersey Mirror*, April 12, 1945.

Additional Reading

"The Comprehensive Management Plan." *New Jersey Pinelands Commission.* nj.gov/pinelands/cmp/summary (accessed December 28, 2007).

Grames, Selwyn Anne. *Historic Tabernacle: A Pictorial Tour.* Tabernacle, NJ: The Tabernacle Historical Society, 1989.

Schmidt, R. Marilyn. *Exploring the Pine Barrens of New Jersey: A Guide.* Chatsworth, NJ: Barnegat Light Press/Pine Barrens Press, 1997.

Solem-Stull, Barbara. *Ghost Towns and Other Quirky Places in the New Jersey Pine Barrens.* Medford, NJ: Plexus Publishing, 2005.

About the Author

Karen F. Riley's initial passion was writing. Nationally published at the age of eleven, her subsequent work has appeared in *New Jersey Monthly*, *Asbury Park Press*, and other media. Her first book, *Whispers in the Pines: The Secrets of Colliers Mills*, deals with the history and environment of the northernmost part of the Pine Barrens. *Voices in the Pines: True Stories from the New Jersey Pine Barrens* brings that history alive through the eyes of the folks who live and work throughout the Pinelands. Karen, her husband, Bill and their three children, Lisa, Laura, and Chris, have lived in New Egypt, NJ, since 1992.

Andrew Gioulis grew up in a family of skilled artisans. He started out as an illustrator and still incorporates sketches into his work as a graphic designer. Andrew has garnered 30 awards for his innovative style and is currently working on his MFA. This book gave him an opportunity to return to the sketchbook to capture the people and places of this unique region. Andrew resides by the Jersey Shore where he can indulge his love of surfing and photography.

Karen and Andrew own KFR Communications, LLC, a custom graphic and website design company located on the fringes of the Pine Barrens. More information on their company can be found at www.kfrcommunications.com. They welcome your feedback on *Voices in the Pines* at info@voicesinthepines.com.

More Great Books
from Plexus Publishing

PIONEER, GO HOME!
By Richard Powell

The novel that might have been called "Piney, Go Home!" delivers a fast-paced story, a terrific cast of characters, and dozens of memorable, laugh-out-loud moments. This 50th anniversary edition restores Richard Powell's New York Times bestseller and includes a previously unpublished preface by the author. Pioneer, Go Home! is a warm and witty tale of little man versus "Big Gummint." Powell relates the adventures of the Kwimpers—a motley clan of New Jersey Pineys who break down on the side of a southern highway project and decide to claim squatter's rights. Call them "hicks" or "bumpkins" if you like, but these Kwimpers are considerably more resourceful than most folks give them credit for—and ten times as stubborn!

280 pp/softbound/ISBN 978-0-937548-71-4/$15.95

A PINE BARRENS ODYSSEY:
A NATURALIST'S YEAR IN THE PINE BARRENS OF NEW JERSEY
By Howard P. Boyd

A Pine Barrens Odyssey is a detailed perspective of the seasons in the Pine Barrens of New Jersey. Primarily focused on the chronology of the natural features of the Pine Barrens, this book is meant as a companion to Howard P. Boyd's A Field Guide to the Pine Barrens of New Jersey.

The two books form an appealing collection for anyone interested in the Pine Barrens of New Jersey. The Field Guide can be used as a reference tool for the types of flora and fauna and the Odyssey as a calendar of what to expect and look for season by season in this beautiful natural area of New Jersey.

275 pp/softbound/ISBN 978-0-937548-34-9/$19.95

PEOPLE OF THE PINES
By Bob Birdsall

Nature photographer Bob Birdsall (Seasons of the Pines) celebrates the people and traditions of the Pine Barrens of New Jersey in this beautifully illustrated volume. Birdsall's perceptive lens and engaging text illumine more than two dozen individuals and their ways of life—many of which are fast vanishing. From "Piney" hunter-gatherers who still live off the land, to hardworking baymen and farmers, volunteers and public servants, artisans and entrepreneurs, scientists, conservationists, and educators, these men and women typify the bold and creative spirit of the region. With roots in the Pines going back 200 years or more, many are deeply committed to preserving tradition, while others are relative newcomers who came to visit and stayed to fight for the future of a wilderness at risk. What the "People of the Pines" share in common—as evidenced by Birdsall's intimate and inspiring portraits—is a boundless passion for this unique and storied land.

160 pp/hardbound/ISBN 978-0-937548-63-9/$39.95

PATRIOTS, PIRATES, AND PINEYS: SIXTY WHO SHAPED NEW JERSEY
By Robert A. Peterson

Southern New Jersey is a region full of rich heritage, and yet it is one of the best kept historical secrets of our nation. Many famous people have lived in Southern New Jersey, and numerous world-renowned businesses were started in this area as well. This collection of biographies provides a history of the area through the stories of such famous figures as John Wanamaker, Henry Rowan, Sara Spenser Washington, Elizabeth Haddon, Dr. James Still, and Joseph Campbell. Some were patriots, some pirates, and some Pineys, but all helped make America what it is today.

168 pp/hardbound/ISBN 978-0-937548-37-0/$29.95
168 pp/softbound/ISBN 978-0-937548-39-4/$19.95

PINELANDS
By Robert Bateman

"A riveting story, written in a style to catch and hold the reader's attention." —Barnegat Bay Banner

"Bateman has written an elegy for one section of New Jersey and for all the places that have been devoured by progress without vision." —The News and Observer (Raleigh, NC)

In a compelling blend of history and fiction, Robert Bateman examines the seductive legacies of the past and how they are used by many to resist the abrasive realities of modern life. With its startling conclusion, Pinelands brings the reader full circle through decades of ambition, violence, love, and decadence to a present that is, perhaps, all too familiar.

256 pp/hardbound/ISBN 978-0-937548-27-1/$21.95
256 pp/softbound/ISBN 978-0-937548-28-8/$12.95

KATE AYLESFORD OR, THE HEIRESS OF SWEETWATER
By Charles J. Peterson
With a new Foreword by Robert Bateman

The legendary historical romance, Kate Aylesford: A Story of Refugees, by Charles J. Peterson, first appeared in 1855, was reissued in 1873 as The Heiress of Sweetwater, and spent the entire 20th century out of print. As readable today as when Peterson first penned it, Kate Aylesford features a memorable cast of characters, an imaginative plot, and a compelling mix of romance, adventure, and history. Plexus Publishing is pleased to return this remarkable novel to print.

306 pp/hardbound/ISBN 978-0-937548-46-2/$22.95